KT-457-757

4th Edition

Reflective Practice in Social Work

Edited by

Christine Knott and
Terry Scragg

Los Angeles | London | New Delhi
Singapore | Washington DC | Melbourne

Series Editors:
Jonathan Parker and Greta Bradley

Learning Matters
An imprint of SAGE Publications Ltd
1 Oliver's Yard
55 City Road
London EC1Y 1SP

SAGE Publications Inc.
2455 Teller Road
Thousand Oaks, California 91320

SAGE Publications India Pvt Ltd
B 1/I 1 Mohan Cooperative Industrial Area
Mathura Road
New Delhi 110 044

SAGE Publications Asia-Pacific Pte Ltd
3 Church Street
#10–04 Samsung Hub
Singapore 049483

Editor: Kate Wharton
Production controller: Chris Marke
Project management: Deer Park Productions,
Tavistock, Devon
Marketing manager: Tamara Navaratnam
Cover design: Wendy Scott
Typeset by: C&M Digitals (P) Ltd, Chennai, India
Printed and bound by CPI Group (UK) Ltd,
  Croydon CRO 4YY

First published in 2007 by Learning Matters. Second
edition published in 2010 by SAGE/Learning Matters.
Third edition published in 2013. Fourth edition
published in 2016.

Library of Congress Control Number: 2015959704

British Library Cataloguing in Publication Data

A catalogue record for this book is available from the
British Library

ISBN 978-1-4739-5210-2 (pbk)
ISBN 978-1-4739-5209-6

Contents

About the editors and contributors

Gill Butler is Emeritus Research Fellow and formerly Deputy Dean (Learning and Teaching), University of Chichester.

Gill Constable was formerly Lecturer in Social Work, Glasgow Caledonian University.

Christine Knott (editor) was formerly Head of Social Work, University of Chichester.

Janet McCray is Professor of Social Care and Workforce Development, Department of Childhood, Social Work and Social Care, University of Chichester.

Andy Mantell is Senior Lecturer, School of Health and Social Care, London South Bank University.

Terry Scragg (editor) is an Independent Practice Educator working with the University of Chichester.

Chris Smethurst is Principal Lecturer in Social Work and Deputy Head, Department of Childhood, Social Work and Social Care, University of Chichester.

Jan Spafford was formerly Principal Lecturer (Learning and Teaching), Department of Childhood, Social Work and Social Care, University of Chichester.

Sandra Wallis is an Independent Consultant and formerly Senior Lecturer in Social Work, Department of Childhood, Social Work and Social Care, University of Chichester.

Acknowledgements

We would like to thank Kate Wharton and Helen Fairlie for their support throughout the work on this new edition.

Introduction

This book is written for the student social worker and explores a range of approaches to reflective practice that will be useful across the whole of your programme of study as well as in subsequent years as you move into practice learning. Experienced and qualified social workers contributing to practice learning will also be able to use this book for consultation, teaching and revision, and to gain an insight into the expectations raised by the qualifying degree in social work. Essentially this book is designed to assist you in developing an understanding of the concept of the reflective practitioner, and in learning how, in conjunction with your practice educator and others, you can take a perspective on your own actions and experiences that have the potential for refining and reframing your practice as a result of these deliberations. Reflection is central to good social work practice, but only if action results from that reflection.

Great emphasis is now placed on developing the skills of reflection about each stage of practice. This has developed over many years in social work, and is not only important during your education to become a social worker, but is also considered key to continued professional development (CPD). As a profession that increasingly acknowledges the value of lifelong learning as a way of keeping up to date, ensuring that research informs practice and honing skills and values for practice, it is important to begin the process at the outset of your development. The importance of reflection as one component of professional development is recognised by its inclusion in the Professional Capabilities Framework and in the Health and Care Professions Council Standards of proficiency for social workers.

Book structure

As you will see below, the book starts with a broad exploration of reflective practice drawing on some of the key texts that have informed the development of the concept and some of the processes that can be adopted in reflective practice. This is then used as the basis for the following chapters that are concerned with aspects of the development of the reflective practitioner from a range of standpoints. Finally, we explore issues of the management of social work practice and interprofessional leadership in the context of reflection.

Part 1 What is reflective practice?

Chapter 1 explores what is meant by reflective practice and some of the potential outcomes from using this technique. The chapter then examines the roots of the concept of reflective practice, with the work of Schön as our starting point, and goes on to discuss its application to social work. The terminology used in reflective practice will be discussed, as will the relationship between evidence-based practice and reflective practice.

The chapter also acknowledges that some environmental conditions in organisations may make reflection more difficult, and that positive relationships and processes need to be in place for constructive reflection to take place.

Chapter 2 examines the methods used when starting the process of reflection. These methods will be familiar to most social work and other professional educators. As a social work student you will find this a key part of the process of learning and teaching on your qualifying programme. This chapter draws on methods that have been discussed in the literature and also practised in both qualifying and post-qualifying social work education. We suggest a wide range of strategies and techniques that you can test out as a way of developing the practical skills of reflection, including how to start the process of reflection and how to maintain a reflective approach as you develop your social work career.

Chapter 3 recognises that the reflective process involves the emotions. This chapter raises important questions about the role of language in both shaping and reflecting dominant discourses in practice. The importance in social work of understanding and processing emotions is then considered, illustrated with reference to child protection practice. An acknowledgement of the emotional component in practice has long been neglected but is now increasingly recognised as helping practitioners understand some of the contradictions and complexities inherent in social work practice. The concept of emotional intelligence is identified as providing a helpful framework for developing emotionally competent practice. A series of reflective tasks is included to support the development of emotional awareness and regulation, which are considered central to the development of emotional intelligence.

Part 2 Developing the reflective practitioner

Chapter 4 focuses on reflection that leads to challenging self-limiting beliefs and promotes action through the use of an approach underpinned by cognitive behaviour therapy. This theory is explained by the use of case studies and their application for social work students as well as work with service users and carers. A number of approaches are considered such as writing reflectively, analysis of self-talk and belief systems, and the use of the ABC technique to challenge self-defeating thoughts. The aim of the chapter is to enable you to develop ideas about how you can reflect in a purposeful manner, which will enable you to problem-solve and develop personal confidence and professional competence.

Chapter 5 highlights the potential pitfalls when applying reflective practice to work with carers. The evolving professional conception of 'the carer' is examined and contrasted with the lived experience of people providing care. Case material is included from research with families where there is a member with Huntington's disease. The chapter goes on to reflect on the participation of service users and carers in social work and the challenging perspective they may bring. An exploration of knowledge, experience and power in understanding and interpretation is included as well as how to use the reflective process to consider other position perspectives and realities.

Social work often involves statutory work with *involuntary* service users, who can be hostile and aggressive. Chapter 6 examines the important role reflective practice can play in these situations as a means of avoiding the risk of social workers reacting in ways that can, albeit unintentionally, actually work to increase the danger for service users and social workers. The process is explained through the concept of professional dangerousness; the chapter provides some useful exercises and concludes with some practical suggestions on how professional dangerousness might be minimised.

Chapter 7 discusses gender in social work, and how the men and woman in social work can be both shaped by socialisation and influenced by others' expectation of gender roles and what are seen as appropriate behaviours for male and female social workers. The chapter explores theories about masculinity and femininity, and some of the tensions you may experience when examining gender differences and attempting to apply them in your practice. The chapter provides you with a range of opportunities to explore gender issues from a personal perspective, in the context of the social work settings and practice situations, and through the use of exercises, case studies and research findings.

Chapter 8 considers reflective practice on placement with a range of suggestions to assist your development as a social worker, with the beneficial outcome of improving your skills in working with service users and carers as well as challenging your assumptions and preconceptions. The chapter has been written to be mainly of relevance to students, although it will also be of interest to practice educators and social workers involved in post-qualifying training and who are completing the ASYE (assessed and supported year in employment).

Part 3 Maintaining reflective practice

Chapter 9 introduces you to the world of management, particularly the work of the front-line manager and some of the tensions inherent in management roles in social work. The case is made in this chapter for managers maintaining a reflective approach to their practice and encouraging a similar approach to the work with the social workers they manage. The second part of this chapter explores how you can actively manage your relationship with your line manager in the context of practice learning so that you can both benefit from the relationship. Lastly, this chapter introduces you to a range of techniques that can be used when reflecting on and about practice.

Finally, Chapter 10 discusses how increasingly social work will be practised in an interprofessional context in complex new organisational structures, with leadership in these new structures essential. This chapter explores the application of a reflective tool to support interprofessional leadership. It builds on previous chapters and themes in relation to the overall concept, critically analysing the use of reflective models in the social care arena. It challenges you to explore how critical evaluation of your own thought and feeling processes, knowledge and experience can support leadership, prevent professional introspection and bring fresh approaches to problem-solving and change in the interprofessional context.

Learning features

This book is interactive and you are encouraged to work through the book as an active participant, taking responsibility for your learning, in order to increase your knowledge, understanding and ability to apply this learning to practice. You will be expected to reflect creatively on how immediate learning needs can be met in the area of assessment, planning, intervention and review and how your professional learning can be developed in your future career. Case studies throughout the book will help you to examine theories and models of reflective practice. We have devised activities that require you to reflect on experiences, situations and events and help you to review and summarise learning undertaken. In this way your knowledge will become deeply embedded as part of your development. When you come to practice learning in an agency, the work and reflection undertaken here will help you to improve and hone your skills and knowledge. This book will introduce knowledge and learning activities for you as a student social worker concerning the central processes relating to issues of reflective practice in all areas of the discipline. Suggestions for further reading are made at the end of each chapter.

This book has been carefully mapped to the new Professional Capabilities Framework for Social Workers in England and will help you to develop the appropriate standards at the right level. These standards are:

- **Professionalism**

  Identify and behave as a professional social worker committed to professional development.

- **Values and ethics**

  Apply social work ethical principles and values to guide professional practice.

- **Diversity**

  Recognise diversity and apply anti-discriminatory and anti-oppressive principles in practice.

- **Rights, justice and economic wellbeing**

  Advance human rights and promote social justice and economic wellbeing.

- **Knowledge**

  Apply knowledge of social sciences, law and social work practice theory.

- **Critical reflection and analysis**

  Apply critical reflection and analysis to inform and provide a rationale for professional decision-making.

- **Intervention and skills**

  Use judgement and authority to intervene with individuals, families and communities to promote independence, provide support and prevent harm, neglect and abuse.

- **Contexts and organisations**

  Engage with, inform, and adapt to changing contexts that shape practice. Operate effectively within your own organisational frameworks and contribute to the development of services and organisations. Operate effectively within multi-agency and interprofessional settings.

- **Professional leadership**

  Take responsibility for the professional learning and development of others through supervision, mentoring, assessing, research, teaching, leadership and management.

References to these standards will be made throughout the text and you will find a diagram of the Professional Capability Framework in Appendix 1 on page 178.

Part 1

What is reflective practice?

Chapter 1

Reflective practice revisited

Christine Knott

A C H I E V I N G   A   S O C I A L   W O R K   D E G R E E

This chapter will help you develop the following capabilities from the Professional Capabilities Framework in the following areas:

- **Professionalism** – Identify and behave as a professional social worker committed to professional development.
- **Knowledge** – Apply knowledge of social science, law and social work practice theory.
- **Critical reflection and analysis** – Apply critical reflection and analysis to inform and provide a rationale for professional decision-making.
- **Values and ethics** – Apply social work ethical principles and values to guide professional practice.

It will also introduce you to the following standards as set out in the 2008 social work subject benchmark statement:

5.1.3   Values and ethics
5.5.2   Gathering information
5.5.3   Analysis and synthesis
5.8   Skills in personal and professional development
6.2   Reflection on performance

This introductory chapter revisits previous writing about reflection, not just in social work but in allied professions too. The main starting point will be to re-examine the work of Donald Schön and subsequent ideas, including depth learning and reflexive practice. Evidence-based practice is also discussed, not in opposition to reflection but hopefully to propose a more integrated approach to social work practice, which necessarily includes both. This links with the idea of relationship-based social work (Ruch et al., 2010) which is founded on the idea that human relationships are of paramount importance and should be at the heart of good social work practice. This book supports an approach to social work that emphasises informed reflection on practice with a service user/worker relationship that is both understanding and supportive.

Social work and social work education moved into a competence-based approach in the late 1980s with the development of the Diploma in Social Work (Dip SW) and then to a task and function approach with the development of National Occupational Standards (NOS) for the Social Work Degree in 2002. The danger of the technical/ rational base for social work practice based on NOS is that it had the potential to lead people to think there are certainties in social work when experience tells practitioners otherwise. National Occupational Standards remained in vogue for all aspects of social work and social care for a number of years and have only recently been superseded by the Professional Capabilities Framework, developed on the recommendations of the Social Work Task Force, established in 2008. The framework is a single set of expectations for social workers at any stage of their career. It acts as a benchmark, ensuring all social work students, educators, practitioners, managers and employers are able to uphold the highest possible standards and deliver the best quality of service.

What is reflective practice?

The terms 'reflection', 'reflective practice' and the 'reflective practitioner' are very current in social work education and practice at both qualifying and continuing professional development (CPD) levels and have been for a number of years. You will also find it very current in the other professions with which social work collaborates to provide the best service for those people who are users of the service, particularly the health professions (Tate and Sills, 2004). While the idea of reflection sounds easy it is far from being so and many writers acknowledge the complexity of the concept. Parker and Bradley (2003) state that social work practice is driven by theory, some taken from formal knowledge that you will learn about on your course, such as attachment theory and theories relating to loss and bereavement. You will also be introduced to knowledge about how to practise using such methods as task-centred, cognitive-behavioural or person-centred approaches, among others. You will be expected to apply these theories to your practice when you are out on assessed practice or indeed when you are a qualified practitioner. What also happens during and after qualification, according to Parker and Bradley, however, is that you also begin to construct a body of informal knowledge, or experiential wisdom from working with people in practice. Reflection and reflective practice help you to integrate theoretical learning, whether formal or informal, into your practice.

Horner (2004), in exploring the question 'What is social work?', considers reflection to be central to good social work practice but only if action results from that reflection, which is known as reflective practice. He considers that reflecting about, on and in practice needs to be developed during initial social work education and is the key to continuing professional development. Hence it is a concept that will underpin post-qualifying training too. He states that a questioning approach that looks in a critical way at thoughts, experiences and practice and seeks to heighten skills as a result of those deliberations is the hallmark of reflection. This message is reiterated in other books in the Transforming Social Work Series (Scragg, in Mantell, 2013). Parker and Bradley (2003) comment on the need for developing a reflective capability, stating that a thoughtful and planned approach will help to make social work clear to service users and also more open to review, so that practice can be improved in the future. This point is taken further by Munro (2011) in her review of child protection. In her report it is recognised that social workers use analytic and intuitive reasoning in their work and together these enable the practitioner to make assumptions that result in decisions based on sound judgements. The link between them is the use of reflection.

At the University of Chichester, where most of the authors were either employed or associated, reflection and reflective practice has been built into the curriculum of all social work and related professional programmes over many years (Ashford et al., 1998). This occurs in a number of ways, which will be explored particularly in the next chapter.

So what is this phenomenon of reflection?

Most of the public service professions are committed to the development of reflective practice. For example, Rolfe et al. (2001) writing about nursing, Tate and Sills (2004) about health professions, and Jennings and Kennedy (1996) writing about education are clear that it is relevant for the development of these professions too. Other writers, including Moon (1999, 2004), take a more generic educational approach so that the concept is valid for a range of professional development activities, not least social work teaching and learning in higher education. Moon (2004) concludes that a common-sense definition of reflection is that it is applied to relatively complicated, ill-structured ideas for which there is not an obvious solution and is largely based on the further processing of knowledge and understanding that we already possess. She suggests that the following outcomes can result from reflective processes:

- learning, knowledge and understanding;
- some form of action;
- a process of critical review;
- personal and continuing professional development;
- reflection on the process of learning or personal functioning (meta-cognition);
- the building of theory from observations in practice situations;
- the making of decisions/resolution of uncertainty, the solving of problems; empowerment and emancipation;
- unexpected outcomes (e.g. images, ideas that could be solutions to dilemmas or seen as creative activity;
- emotion (that can be an outcome or can be part of the process);
- clarification and the recognition that there is a need for further reflection.

(Moon, 2004, p84)

Think of an interaction that happened recently on your course, either in class or in practice, and analyse it from the above list of outcomes. What was the main outcome for you?

Comment

It may be that your reflection centred on thoughts, feelings or actions. It does not matter which, but on a relatively simple level most of us can reflect back to a situation and find some further meaning about it: either what we were thinking or feeling or what action resulted.

Moon's list above equates closely with the critical reflection and analysis domain of the Professional Capabilities Framework which outlines the following:

- use of critical thinking;
- use of multiple sources of knowledge and evidence;
- application of creativity and curiosity;
- creation of hypotheses;
- having a rationale for judgements and decisions;

    based on adult learning theory.

However, in a thought-provoking social work article, Ixer (1999) makes the case in the title for there being no such thing as reflection. He considers that often uncritical attention has been paid to developing and assessing reflective practice in social work education. He finds definitions of reflection and reflective practice to be problematic and theoretical explanations open to debate. *We do not know enough about reflection or how intricate and complex cognitive processes can enhance learning to be able to assess it fairly. Much of what is assessed remains speculative and conjectural* (Ixer, 1999, p522). In this book we aim to share what we have discovered about the nature of reflection in a number of areas relevant to social work and how reflective practice can be maintained in the ever-changing context in which qualified social workers practise.

Roots of reflective practice

So where has the notion of reflection and reflective practice come from? Writers taking a historical approach to the development of ideas on reflective practice generally go back to the work of educational philosopher John Dewey, writing in the inter-war period (Dewey 1933, 1938). His view was that people only begin to reflect when there is a problem to be solved (see Moon, above). This is very familiar for social work. Dewey thinks that reflection is the continual re-evaluation of personal beliefs, assumptions and ideas in the light of experience and data and the generation of alternative interpretations of those experiences and data.

The starting point for this revisiting, however, begins later with the work of such adult educationalists as Donald Schön (1983, 1987, 2002) writing about the reflective practitioner, and the work of Steven Brookfield (1987) writing about critical thinking and the associated idea of critical learning. Schön advocated two types of reflection: reflection-on-action and reflection-in-action. So, first, *reflection-on-action* is thinking back on something already done, away from the action, starting with recall and a description of what happened. This is what Activity 1.1 asked you to do. Reflection-on-action then moves to a fuller examination of the experience initially using who, what, where, when, why and how type questions. The process therefore aims to transform the experience into knowledge, which is different from just thinking about practice, which is merely recall without learning from it.

The idea of the *lens* here may be helpful in trying to understand the experience being reflected upon. What frame of reference (or lens) is being used to make sense of what has happened? What theories are being applied to this situation? It is easy to reinforce previously held opinions about people and situations which may lead to prejudice and discriminatory practice if we do not recognise what we are using to make sense of reflections. It is also important to recognise what we are feeling as we reflect on the experience. Are the feelings positive or negative? For example, did you feel anxious or confident or satisfied or disappointed? When someone who wears glasses puts them on, the difference in being able to see clearly is immense. Things come into focus and clearer patterns emerge. This is what reflection-on-action can begin to achieve for the beginning professional practitioner. So it is essentially a retrospective activity, thinking about an event after it has taken place. 'Hindsight is wonderful' is a phrase that is often heard. It can be summarised as a process of transforming experience into knowledge and understanding, rather than a process of skill acquisition. There is clearly a strong cognitive element to this process but there is also a feeling/affective process, which also needs to be included in the reflective process. Remembrance and recognition of feelings that were uppermost is an important element in the reflective process, although the facilitation of such reflection needs to be undertaken sensitively.

ACTIVITY **1.2**

Reflect back to a recent practice experience, either simulated on your course or actual, and describe the lens that you used to make sense of what you observed. What feelings were uppermost for you?

Comment

There are a number of techniques that can be used to enhance this process of reflection-on-action. Some involve talking, either one to one or in a small group, writing, other creative activities, again either on your own, with another or in a group. As social workers we need to become familiar with the process of reflection and you will find it a fundamental process at both qualifying and post-qualifying levels. Learning from experience and by experience is an essential element of social work training both in class and practice. Some of these initiating activities to stimulate reflection will be explored in more detail in the following chapter.

Schön's second type of reflection he calls *reflection-in-action*, or thinking about what you are doing while you are doing it, having a 'feel' for something and doing something about it. This way of practising is the more important form of reflection for experienced professional practitioners. It is probably more relevant to qualified social workers under-taking post-qualifying training. This is a model that celebrates the intuitive and artistic approaches that can be applied to uncertain and shifting, swampy situations. Schön (1991) advocates the development of a practice artistry rather than a technical solu-tion to deal with the *indeterminate swampy zones of practice involving uncertainty, uniqueness and value conflict*. This is so familiar to social work practice and is essential if you are to work effectively with the people who use services and the learning that results from effective engagement. It can be considered as an intuitive reflectivity, where thinking and acting go together, as one is practising. Associated with this is the idea of *knowing in action or theories in use*, which describes the knowledge that is shown in practice, which is not described beforehand. The idea of professional artistry as opposed to technical competence is debated below, as it is not without its critics.

In addition it is important that social workers pause before action to give them-selves time to think and hopefully avoid errors. This we can call *reflection-for-action*. Thompson and Thompson (2008) explore this and advise that it can help in anticipat-ing possible difficulties and thus give the social worker a greater sense of confidence and control, with a positive effect on morale and motivation.

As well as the lens by which we make sense of our reflections, mentioned above, this is where the addition of the metaphor of the *mirror* may be helpful, as the mirror reflects back to us what is going on for us in tricky situations. It also helps us to recognise what we are feeling as well as thinking. A good tutor/mentor/practice teacher/assessor as well as fellow students and service users and carers can facilitate this mirroring process, or clear reflecting back. Good feedback can aid learning during an experience as well as afterwards. So it is relevant for reflection-in-action as well as reflection-on-action.

Moon (2004) raises the following interesting discussion points:

- Emotion is central to the reflective process.

- Reflection is always about 'my own' processes (i.e. always in the first person).

- Some people cannot reflect.

ACTIVITY *1.3*

What do you think about the above points raised by Moon? Are you encouraged to express emotion in your written work? Are you encouraged to write in the first person? Is reflection a universal attribute or is it a learned skill?

Comment

Generally you will be required to write in the third person on your social w
programmes. However, we consider it appropriate to use the first person if
are writing reflectively on your own experience. We would expect all social v
students to be able to reflect on their practice. To us it is the hallmark of a pro
sional practitioner. Regarding emotions, Munro (2011) recognises that there i
important emotional dimension in how social workers reason and act. It is im
tant to recognise both your own emotions and those of others involved, espe
the service user.

Depth learning

Jenny Moon (2004) has an interesting chapter on the depth quality of reflective learning, which potentially introduces the idea of levels of learning, or in other words, a
potential hierarchy of reflection. This seems to be logical so that ways of developing
deeper learning and reflection appear to resonate with development – in academic
terms, from first-year undergraduate level to post-qualifying/post graduate level/
master's level. From the adult education literature, deep reflection is associated with
Mezirow's (1992) concept of perspective transformation. It may also resonate with
ideas about the development of professional practitioners from novice to expert. The
novice is characterised by adherence to taught rules and little discretionary judgement, while the expert is characterised by freedom from rules and guidelines with an
intuitive grasp of situations, based on deep understanding, knowing what is possible,
using analytical approaches in novel situations or when new problems occur. Thus
the expert stage is characterised by implicit and unconscious practice. Interestin[g]'
this can also be applied to the competence model of development from unconscic
incompetence, to conscious incompetence, to conscious competence and finally to
unconscious competence.

Higher education is very familiar with levels, with the publication of the Qualit[y]
Assurance Agency Framework for Higher Education Qualifications (FHEQ) with associated learning outcomes and assessment criteria with which you, as students, will be
only too familiar.

The taxonomy of learning in the cognitive domain is also relevant too. So learning
goes from knowledge to understanding to application to analysis to synthesis to evaluation. A more gender-based approach on the development of knowledge is that of
Belenky et al. (1987), which goes from silence to constructed knowledge. The meta-
cognitive process is therefore supported by models of learning, which facilitate the
reflective process. When it comes to practice, fewer models of a taxonomy or hierarchical nature exist. The Professional Capabilities Framework has nine capabilities
(domains), which are relevant regardless of levels of experience, and so provides a single comprehensive set of expectations of social workers at each stage of their career.
The framework also has nine levels, from entry to social work training to the strategic
social work level. This book is mostly concerned with initial qualification and Assessed
and Supported Year in Employment (ASYE).

i do not
w

My per
plan w

Evidence-based practice and reflective practice

Another term that is commonly used in professional social work education is 'evidence-based practice'. It may be that your university course favours one approach above the other as they can be argued to be in opposition to each other because in their most extreme forms they foster entirely different ways of developing and using theory in practice (Healy, 2005, p97). Evidence-based practice relies on rational knowledge to inform practice that has been tested through scientific methods. In Schön's language it is technical/rational rather than intuitive artistry (Schön, 1987). It may be entitled empirical practice (Reid, 1994). Healy argues that it is probably better to think about evidence-based practice and reflective practice as a continuum rather than as an opposition. The social work professional needs to be able to articulate the effectiveness of proposed interventions, or ways of working with people who use services, based on empirical research. This is particularly so where difficult judgements are being made, for example in work involving child protection and mental health.

The evidence-based approach is to be found in other professions, particularly in the health and criminal justice arenas. So as multi-professional work is increasingly advocated it is important that social workers in training recognise and value the approach from which other colleagues may be operating. Increasingly, employing organisations, both statutory and independent, service users and carers and the general public want to be clear on what research and knowledge basis decisions are made.

Healy (2005) argues that evidence-based practice is essentially a top-down approach to theory development and its application. In other words, social workers are the subject and users of knowledge, not the makers of it. The separation of knowledge development from its application in practice means that social workers do not have the time or the scientific tools to develop robust theories of practice and have little opportunity to question how the knowledge was developed or how it might be challenged in practice. By contrast, the reflective approach recognises the value of the practitioner's lived experience of practice as a basis for making and using knowledge in practice. It respects the specificity of each service user's unique situation. Social work is a messy occupation, which involves perceptions and feelings as well as material facts (Parton, 2001). However, reflective practice, which uses the social worker's reflections as the basis of knowledge creation and use, is also problematic. The emphasis on tacit or intuitive knowledge above knowledge from an evidence base means that it will be inaccessible to other colleagues, service users and carers, employers and funding agencies. So both approaches are open to criticism. This may lead to confusion for social workers in training too. The view that is taken at Chichester is that both approaches are valuable but some integration is necessary. Students need to be clear where the information informing their practice comes from. If it is purely based on their own subjective reflections, then it needs to be informed by evidence. A question frequently asked both verbally and on written work is: *Where is your evidence for that?* If the information is only based on evidence from research then students will be asked to reflect on the research and find meaning relevant to themselves and the practice situation. Thus we promote the concept of the *informed reflective practitioner*.

What is reflexive practice?

Taylor and White define reflexivity as:

> *an elusive term often used interchangeably with reflection. It encompasses reflection but also incorporates other features so that it is not just the individualised action of separate practitioners in the manner suggested by reflective practice, rather it is the collective action of an academic discipline or occupational group. For workers in health and welfare it means that they subject knowledge claims and practice to analysis.*

(2000, p206)

So it could be argued that reflexive practice is just another way of describing practice that is more like Schön's reflection-in-action, but generally reflexion is not just concerned with an interior individualistic humanistic process but involves iteration with exterior social and political processes. This, of course, is the essential differentiating element of social work from the other professions. Social workers 'work the social' (Parton, 2001). Reflection of itself does not lead to 'good enough' professional practice. It needs to be tested against agreed standards for that profession. It could equally be argued that having a Code of Ethics does not of itself lead to ethical practice. Indeed, those social workers involved in statutory social work have to deal with many ethical issues arising from the increasingly bureaucratic, managerial context in which they are required to practise. The role of the state has changed from one of provider of welfare to vulnerable people to one of commissioner and regulator. The case could be made that the needs of managers are privileged over the needs of service users and carers. The reflective practitioner therefore needs to be able to place their reflections-on-and-in-and-for-action in the social arena of social policy and economics.

Critical thinking

The term 'critical' also appears to be important, so that reflection needs to be critical, involving critical thinking and critical self-awareness and leading to ethical practice. According to Paul and Elder (2005) of the Foundation for Critical Thinking, a critical thinker is capable of:

- raising vital questions and problems, clearly and precisely;
- gathering and assessing relevant information, using theories and ideas to interpret it effectively;
- reaching conclusions and solutions, tested against relevant criteria;
- thinking open-mindedly, owning assumptions and consequences;
- communicating effectively.

Brown and Rutter (2006), in their book on critical thinking for social work, explore the intellectual resources that are needed for critical thinking as follows:

- background knowledge;
- critical concepts;
- critical thinking standards;
- strategies;
- habits of mind.

A simpler way of expressing this is in Smith's (1992) three key factors of knowledge, authority and willingness to doubt.

Brown and Rutter argue that *the skills of critical thinking allow the best quality decisions or actions possible for the situations we encounter* (2006, p10). This capability is definitely needed in social work practice.

Ethical issues

The other aspect that seems to be involved in developing the critical reflective practitioner is the awareness of ethical issues or value conflicts and the potential, as there is in any relationship or process, for oppression. Taylor (2000), writing about facilitating public/private reflection, recognises that it can generate difficult feelings with painful personal experiences being reactivated. Brown and Rutter (2006) make a similar point that the process of critical thinking can be threatening, provoke anxiety and create adverse reactions from other people. They advise people to seek support if the negative aspects are adversely affecting them. This applies both to the educational setting as well as to the practice setting. So the process of critical thinking and thus critical reflection needs support. This is where a tutor in the educational setting and a practice educator/ supervisor in the practice setting are crucial. If this support is not forthcoming then there is the ethical question as to the level to which critical reflection should be encouraged. Recognition of feelings (see above) therefore is an important part of critical reflection. There is some evidence that men find it harder to engage in reflection than women (Moon, 2004, p93). Men and social work will be discussed further in a later chapter.

All experiential learning has an element of risk as the responsibility for the level of engagement passes from the tutor/mentor to the students in learning environments and from the practice educator/assessor in the practice environment. Guidance should be given about the potential for distress, either from the nature of the reflected upon material or the actual process of reflection.

Ixer makes the important point that:

> Social work has become steeped in demands that students should demonstrate reflection in practice as a learning outcome. The danger this poses to vulnerable learners in the assessment relationship, when assessors' own conceptions of reflection may be

*poorly formed and may not match those of their students, is worryingly likely to com-
pound the imbalance of power between them ... Until such time as we can state more
clearly what it is, we have to accept that there is no theory of reflection that can be
adequately assessed.*

(1999, p513)

In a thought-provoking article Yip (2006) strikes a note of caution about self-
reflection in reflective practice. Yip agrees that under appropriate conditions
reflection can be constructive and result in self-enhancement. However, the
pertinent point is made that under inappropriate conditions it can be highly
destructive to a social worker's self-development. The inappropriate conditions
may include such things as an oppressive social environment at work/placement
which could include a highly critical supervisor, apathetic colleagues, and a
demanding working environment, which includes a demanding workload. The
development of a trusting relationship with the practice educator and the supervisor in the workplace is essential for reflection to take place honestly and openly so
that learning and professional practice is enhanced. Disclosure of learning needs
and practice difficulties must not be misused so that the student/worker feels
undermined and/or exploited. As stated above, reflection is a powerful process
and requires mutual respect on all parties. Perhaps more seriously, reflection may
uncover unresolved past traumas from childhood, family and partner relationships.
Under these circumstances, where physical and mental health issues are apparent
Yip argues that self-reflection in reflective practice may create more harm than
good. The clear message is that appropriate conditions need to be in place for
constructive reflection to take place.

This book is attempting to add to that clarification so that both the process and outcome of reflection can be more clearly taught and assessed.

CHAPTER SUMMARY

There is no doubt that the terminology around reflection, reflexivity and reflective practice is difficult and
that some educators and practitioners will favour one interpretation above another. We would argue that an
integration of both the reflective and evidence-based approaches to learning and practice are needed and
that they are not necessarily mutually exclusive. Social workers need to be informed reflective practitioners.
They need to know from research which interventions are most likely to lead to the best outcomes. In other
words, 'What Works', but not to be limited by that as social work research is relatively in its infancy and
some of it is contradictory. The establishment of the Social Care Institute for Excellence (SCIE) was a move in
the right direction for the recognition and funding of social work and social care research and its dissemina-
tion. The aim of SCIE is to improve the experience of people who use social care services by developing and
promoting knowledge about good practice in social care. Social workers also need to continually develop
their capacity for reflection so that they are aware of what sort of practitioner they are and how effective
they are in their practice. Supervisors and managers need to create an appropriate environment in which
reflection can occur to good effect.

FURTHER READING

Healy, K (2005) *Social work theories in context: Creating frameworks for practice*. Basingstoke: Palgrave Macmillan.

Moon, J (2004) *A handbook of reflective and experiential learning: Theory and practice*. London: Routledge Falmer.

Ruch, G, Turney, D, and Ward, A (eds) (2010) *Relationship-based social work: Getting to the heart of practice*. London: Jessica Kingsley.

Schön, D (2002) From technical rationality to reflection-in-action. In R Harrison, F Reeve, A Hanson and J Clarke (eds), *Supporting lifelong learning. Volume 1: Perspectives on learning*. London: Routledge/Open University.

Yip, K (2006) Self-reflection in reflective practice: a note of caution. *British Journal of Social Work*, 36: 777–88.

REFERENCES

Ashford, D, Blake, D and Knott, C (1998) Changing conceptions of reflective practice. *Journal of Interprofessional Care*, 12 (1).

Belenky, M, Clinchy, B, Goldberger, N and Tarule, J (1987) *Women's ways of knowing: The development of self, voice and mind*. New York: Basic Books.

Brookfield, S (1987) *Developing critical thinkers*. Buckingham: Open University Press.

Brown, K and Rutter, L (2006) *Critical thinking for social work*. Exeter: Learning Matters.

Dewey, J (1933) *How we think*. Boston: D.C. Heath.

Dewey, J (1938) *Logic: The theory of inquiry*. Troy, MN: Reinhart and Winston.

Healy, K (2005) *Social work theories in context: Creating frameworks for practice*. Basingstoke: Palgrave Macmillan.

Horner, N (2004) *What is social work? Context and perspectives*. Exeter: Learning Matters.

Ixer, G (1999) There's no such thing as reflection. *British Journal of Social Work*, 29(6): 13–27.

Jennings, C and Kennedy, E (1996) *The reflective professional in education*. London: Jessica Kingsley.

Mezirow, J and Karlovic, LN (1992) Fostering critical reflection in adulthood: a guide to transformative and emancipatory learning. *Canadian Journal for the Study of Adult Education*, 6(1): 86–89.

Moon, J (1999) *Reflection in learning and professional development: Theory and practice*. London: Kogan Page.

Moon, J (2004) *A handbook of reflective and experiential learning: Theory and practice*. London: Routledge Falmer.

Munro, E (2011) *The Munro review of child protection: Final report – A child-centred system*. London: Department of Education. Available at: www.education.gov.uk/publications/eOrderingDownload/Munro-Review.pdf.

Parker, J and Bradley, G (2003) *Social work practice: Assessment, planning, intervention and review*. Exeter: Learning Matters.

Parton, N (2001) The current state of social work in UK universities: some personal reflections. *Social Work Education*, 20: 167–74.

Paul, R and Elder, L (2005) *A miniature guide to critical thinking: Concepts and tools.* The Foundation for Critical Thinking. Available at: www.criticalthinking.org.

Reid, W (1994) The empirical practice movement. *Social Service Review*, 69: 165–84.

Rolfe, G, Freshwater, D and Jasper, M (2001) *Critical reflection for nursing and the helping professions.* Basingstoke: Palgrave Macmillan.

Ruch, G, Turney, D and Ward, A (eds) (2010) *Relationship-based social work: Getting to the heart of practice.* London: Jessica Kingsley.

Schön, D (1983) *The reflective practitioner. How professionals think in action.* London: Temple Smith.

Schön, D (1987) *Educating the reflective practitioner.* San Francisco: Jossey-Bass.

Schön, D (1991) *The reflective turn: Case studies in and on educational practice.* New York: Teachers Press Columbia University.

Schön, D (2002) From technical rationality to reflection-in-action. In R Harrison, F Reeve, A Hanson and J Clarke (eds), *Supporting lifelong learning. Volume One. Perspectives on learning.* London: Routledge/ Open University.

Scragg, T (2013) Reflective practice. In A Mantell (ed.), *Skills for Social Work Practice*, 2nd edition. London: Sage/Learning Matters.

Smith, F (1992) *To think in language, learning and education.* London: Routledge.

Tate, S and Sills, M (eds) (2004) *The development of critical reflection in the health professions.* London: Higher Education Academy.

Taylor, BJ (2000) *Reflective Practice: A guide for nurses and midwives.* Buckingham: Open University Press.

Taylor, C and White, S (2000) *Practising reflexivity in health and welfare: Making knowledge.* Buckingham: Open University Press.

Thompson, S and Thompson, N (2008) *The critically reflective practitioner.* Basingstoke: Palgrave Macmillan.

Yip, K (2006) Self-reflection in reflective practice: a note of caution. *British Journal of Social Work*, 36: 777–88.

Chapter 2
Getting Started

Christine Knott and Jan Spafford

Introduction

This chapter links with the previous chapter and offers some useful and practical ways to develop your skills of reflection. Most social work courses at qualifying and post-qualifying levels will require you to complete reflective pieces of work, which will be assessed. Some may form part of your assessment of the professional practice elements of your course and others will be part of your learning and assessment of university-based elements. Many students find this process of reflection difficult to grasp but once the process has been developed it will underpin your learning about the theory and practice of social work while you are students and on into your life as a qualified social worker. So the earlier you address and value the process of reflection the better. It will also underpin your continuing professional development as a social worker, which is a requirement for continuing registration. When you continue into post-qualifying studies you will also be required to enhance your reflective capabilities. In terms of interprofessional work, most other professions with whom you will work, such as the health professions and teaching, also value the process of reflection as part of their professional and post-professional education and training.

The framework for this chapter starts with understanding how we learn and some models of learning from experience. If the reflective practitioner is a worker who is able to use experience and theory to guide and inform practice, then that is what we consider they need to experience on their qualifying course. Reflection involves being open-minded, carefully thinking things through; it can be a source of constant learning rather than a rigid, routinised approach to practice (Thompson, 2009).

Getting started on any activity is for some of us the hardest part. However, once we have got going we wonder what all the fuss was about. Getting started on this chapter was a challenge for the authors. We arranged to meet away from work at one of our homes. We began with coffee and a chat. Before we knew it, it was lunchtime and so we did not really get down to reviewing what we had prepared for quite a few hours. Once we began to work the ideas flowed and we had a productive time. The avoidance of getting started is known as displacement activity. Instead of getting on with the required activity we do all sorts of other things, like having a cup of coffee, putting a load into the washing machine and then having another cup of coffee and so on. We call it the 'I'll just' syndrome. We say to ourselves, 'I'll just take the dog for a walk' or 'I'll just have a bath', etc. Extreme displacement can find us doing those things that we would avoid doing in normal circumstances, such as cleaning the oven or sorting out the mess in the garage. We can all experience blocks to reflection and so to learning. A useful early activity is to reflect on experiences that have enhanced or blocked learning.

ACTIVITY **2.1**

Make a list of three good and three poor learning experiences. What happened that helped your learning and what happened that blocked your learning? Where possible share the results of this activity with a colleague on the course, your tutor and/or practice assessor.

Comment

This activity provides a solid foundation for beginning the process of learning how to learn and reflecting on your preferred way of learning. This will be a continuing theme throughout this chapter. It is sometimes helpful to realise that you are not the only person who finds that learning can be both enhancing and difficult. It is useful to share our previous experiences of learning. It is also important for those who are employed to facilitate our learning, both academic and from practice, to be aware of what we find helpful to that process. Finally it is up to each of us to begin to take responsibility for our own learning and to try and deal with or avoid those experiences that block our learning.

In completing this activity Susan, a year one student, realised that there had been a number of times during a lecture when she found it hard to listen, take notes and understand what she was hearing. She always had to go away and spend time reading over her notes and still felt she did not fully understand. On reflection she recognised that if she had prior access to the lecture notes she would learn better. So she approached the lecturer and asked if it was possible to have the lecture notes before the session. The lecturer agreed to post the lecture notes on the intranet a few days before each lecture. Susan then found with the opportunity to read ahead she was able to participate more fully in any discussion. Many of the other students were also grateful to Susan for making this request.

Reflective space

The idea of a reflective space is an important one for us. By this we mean both a physical space and the time to spend in it. A reflective space requires organisation and negotiation. Some of your social work courses will have negotiated this for you so far as your academic work is concerned. Study time will hopefully have been timetabled and space in university learning resource centres is there to be used. Of course, some of your own time will be needed too. Ideally on placement a desk and regular supervision will form part of placement agreement meetings/contracts so that a reflective space is available there too, although this may not always be possible. It is important that the same negotiation and organisation occurs in your domestic lives if you are to benefit from reflective activities. The level and amount of negotiation will vary according to your circumstances. If you are living in shared accommodation such as a shared student house, or with a partner and/or children, then it is very important to make your needs known and agreed. We recognise that a reflective space may sometimes be part of another activity such as having a bath or a shower, doing household tasks, waiting for a bus or a train. These sorts of spaces can be used productively and are often free of potential learning blocks that can be evoked by sitting at a desk. It helps us to realise how often we do in fact engage in reflection. Some of these activities may be seen as part of a ritual that marks the beginning of a reflective process. Adams (1990) explores the idea that reflective work, writing or thinking benefits from a few minutes of focused quieting at the beginning.

It is probably more challenging to secure a reflective space from work on post-qualifying social work courses but it is worth the effort to negotiate time and space from your line manager as it will be in your agency's interests that you enhance your learning and practice capabilities as a post-qualified practitioner.

Experiment with finding something that helps you to enter a different space to begin your reflection, for example a few minutes with your eyes closed, deep breathing, arranging your space to suit yourself, having a cup of tea, or wearing a particular item of clothing.

Comment

This activity will help you to put on your 'thinking cap'. Over time you will find what works best for you. This may change depending on your mood, time of day and what you want to accomplish.

Experiential learning and the learning cycle

Most social work courses will use experiential learning techniques such as role play and simulation. So what are the components of learning by and from experience? Jenny Moon says:

> in general terms, the distinguishing features of experiential learning are that it refers to the organising and construction of learning from observations that have been made in some practical situation, with the implication that the learning can then lead on to action (or improved action).

(1999, p20)

Reflection is thus presumed to have a key role in experiential learning or in enabling experiential learning. On your qualifying social work course over half of the course is spent in professional practice and probably quite a high proportion of university learning and teaching will also employ teaching methods that seek to value the experience you bring with you and create new/simulated experiences. Skills laboratories will facilitate experiential learning. Generally such laboratories will have audio-visual equipment so that skills of good communication can be recorded and reflected upon. A good starting point is with an audio tape.

ACTIVITY 2.3

Using a recorder, begin by reading a short paragraph from a book. Once you have got the settings right, record your response to the following questions and try to be as relaxed and conversational as possible:

- *What did I enjoy most on the course today?*

- *What learning stood out for me?*

- *What did I find uncomfortable or difficult?*

Comment

You may find that some important learning on the course does not happen in class but as a result of an informal interaction or incident that you were part of. Reflection on situations can help you to learn how you respond and also how you might wish you had responded. As you become more confident in using recordings you can then try recording a more conversational exchange with another student.

Models of learning

A major model of learning that you may encounter is the Kolb Learning Cycle.

Kolb's (1984) learning cycle includes the following concepts:

- concrete experience;

- observations and reflections;

- formation of abstract concepts and generalisations;

- testing implications of concepts in new situations.

Kolb makes the case that in order to be effective learners the above four kinds of ability are needed, which match the four stages of the learning cycle, namely concrete experiencing of a situation, reflective observation, abstract conceptualisation and active experimentation. This whole idea of using reflection to turn experience into learning has been the subject of a number of books, not least that by Boud et al. (1985). They see experiential learning operating both within the classroom and outside the classroom in professional practice. We would definitely concur with that conclusion. Boyd and Fales (1983), coming from an adult education and counselling perspective, see reflection as the key element in learning from experience in such a way that they are cognitively or affectively changed. The area of feeling and emotion is the focus of Chapter 3.

Learning styles

Following on from Kolb's learning cycle, a number of self-evaluation questionnaires have been developed to help you explore what 'type' of learner you are. They tend to form part of study skills programmes and most social work courses will include this aspect of helping their students understand their preferences, styles and habits. Cottrell (2003) summarises and includes some of these questionnaires which students may like to access. At Chichester we have used one adapted from Kolb's work and also made reference to the work of Honey and Mumford (2006). Their terminology is similar to that of Kolb, as follows:

Activists prefer to work in an intuitive, flexible and spontaneous way, generating ideas and trying out new things. They usually have lots to say and contribute. They like to learn from experience, such as through problem-based learning, working in groups, workshops, discussion and teamwork.

Reflectors prefer to watch and reflect, gathering data and taking time to consider all options and alternatives before making a decision. They prefer to learn through lectures, project work and working alone.

Theorists prefer to learn by going through things thoroughly and logically, step by step with clear guidelines, and have to feel they have learnt solidly before they apply what they know. They prefer to learn from books, problem-based learning and discussion.

Pragmatists prefer to learn by 'trying things out' to see if they work, just getting on with it, getting to the point. They like to be practical and realistic. They prefer to learn on work-based projects and practical applications.

ACTIVITY 2.4

Look at the learning preferences as described above and decide which type best describes you and whether the associated way of learning matches your preferences.

Comment

You may have recognised that you have a preference for learning in a particular way and that may be a good starting point for you. You will need, however, to develop the other styles as most teachers will have a preference for teaching from a particular style, although good teachers will vary their methods so that all students can be engaged in the learning. Honey and Mumford (2006) offer a list of suggestions of exercises that will help you develop the full range of learning styles and thus become more competent learners.

CASE STUDY

Swaati, a very confident active student, always volunteered for role play and other experiential activities in class. However, she gradually realised that other students were learning more from the activity than she was. After completing a learning style questionnaire she recognised that her reflector style needed some development. Consequently she began to pay more attention to recording thoughts and feelings and taking part in the post-activity discussion. She then began to make more sense of the theoretical material given out by the tutor and make more sense of her learning from practice. In this way she had completed the learning cycle. She realised that she did not need to lead in role play and could learn by observing and listening to others.

What follows in this chapter are some of the activities that may be used on your social work course, in the order that they are generally experienced. These activities may vary as we recognise that they can operate at different depths of learning.

Personal development planning (PDP)

All university students are being encouraged/required to undertake some form of PDP self-evaluation, and Cottrell (2003) is very helpful in this respect. Many social work courses have used self-evaluation techniques for many years based on the premise that you need to know yourself before you try to know and work with other people in any deep or meaningful way. As stated above, Cottrell advocates starting early on reflection as part of a lifelong skill. She considers that the process of reflection has a number of elements as follows:

- making sense of the experience;
- standing back;
- repetition;
- deeper honesty;
- weighing up;
- clarity;
- understanding;
- making judgements.

Some of the activities in this chapter relate more closely to some of these elements than others.

Similarly Thompson (2009) in the chapter on reflective practice asserts that reflection is the essential process in applying theory to practice, and lists the following activities as being essential to the promotion of reflective practice:

Reading: Time spent reading is an investment and is not just for students but for all practitioners to give a broader perspective. After all, you are all social work students who are reading for a degree and it is essential to read before writing.

Asking: First, this applies to what you are reading so that you can make sense of what might be written in a jargonistic or academic style. It is also important to ask questions of tutors and each other and practitioners. Asking good questions is a vital skill for social workers. A social work assessment requires asking questions in a way that enhances engagement with people who use the services and their carers and other professionals involved.

Watching: There is much to be learned from an enhanced level of awareness in terms of observational skills and being sensitive to what is happening around us. Again this is explored in more detail below and in Chapter 3.

Feeling: The emotional dimension of work with people must not be underestimated, and thinking and feeling need to be synthesised in reflective practice. Chapter 3 explores this further.

Talking: Sharing views and ideas about social work and social work practice encourages a broader perspective and a chance to learn from others' experiences. Constructive dialogue assists in broadening horizons, deepening understanding and enhancing skills.

Thinking: A thoughtful approach to practice is essential if you are not to become routinised, which Thompson regards as a dangerous way of dealing with sensitive issues. Time pressures equally can militate against thinking carefully about actions (see Chapter 1).

Learning logs or journals

One of the most common ways of developing reflective practice used on social work courses is the use of learning logs or learning journals, so we will make this an early activity for getting started. Subsequent chapters also make reference to this important activity. We use the term 'learning journal' although we appreciate that a variety of terminology may be used. The use of reflective journals is not restricted to professional courses and we have heard of their use on such diverse undergraduate degrees as theology and media studies. The purposes of writing reflective journals are varied but may, according to Moon (1999), include some of the following:

- to record experience;
- to develop learning in ways that enhance other learning;
- to deepen the quality of learning;
- to enable the learner to understand their own learning process;
- to facilitate learning from experience;
- to increase active involvement in learning;
- to increase the ability to reflect and improve the quality of learning;
- to enhance problem-solving skills;
- as a means of assessment;
- to enhance professional practice;
- to explore the self, personal constructs and understand one's view of the world;
- to enhance the valuing of the self towards self-empowerment;
- for therapeutic purposes or as a means towards behaviour change;
- as a means of slowing down learning, taking a more thorough account of a situation or situations;
- to enhance creativity by making better use of intuitive understanding;
- to free up writing and the representation of learning;
- to provide an alternative voice for those not good at expressing themselves;
- to foster reflective and creative interaction in a group.

You may have already discovered that some of your reflections might be difficult, possibly painful or upsetting. You may have tried to block or censor these reflections. As discussed in Chapter 1, it is important that this is shared either in supervision or tutorial.

Guidance about the writing of journals may vary. On social work courses journals may be required to follow a particular structure or they may be totally unstructured. Our experience is that students prefer structured guidance in the early stages but then develop their own style and structure. Essentially, journals start off being rather descriptive but may quite quickly move to being more critically analytical about an event. Once the essential elements of a situation are described, then this can be followed by some form of self-evaluation of personal experience, strengths, qualities and skills. Sometimes journals themselves are assessed, or particular selections from the journal are included in the form of a journal analysis. This means that the students can remove those sections that are more private. They may, however, be shared in a tutorial or practice supervision.

Cottrell (2003) makes the important point that keeping a reflective journal can be very challenging, especially being motivated to making regular entries. It requires determination, good planning and a far-sighted approach. Being convinced of the value of the journal is paramount. It may be an overused process on some social work courses. Some useful exercises for getting started can include the following from Moon (1999), which draw quite heavily on the work of Progoff (1975):

- writing from different angles;
- metaphor;
- unsent letters;
- reflection on a book or reading assignment;
- using a critical friend;
- responding to set questions;
- describing the process of solving problems;
- focusing on a past experience;
- making lists;
- stepping stones from earliest memories;
- period reflections;
- imaginary dialogues with people;
- dialogues with events and projects;
- working with dreams and imagery.

It might be helpful to have a go at one or two of these to see if they help you to get started on journal writing. Alternatively try the next activity.

ACTIVITY 2.5

On your own: Spend about 10–15 minutes composing a letter to a previous teacher or tutor, giving them positive feedback about how you experienced them in that role. Include your feelings and any outcomes of this experience; for example, you inspired me to read Jane Austen, to think about working with people, etc.

With another student: Swap letters with your partner and take it in turns to role play being the recipient of the letter and meeting the writer to discuss it.

Comment

This activity builds on Activity 2.1 and enables you to be more concrete and specific about a previous learning experience and leads you to explore the consequences and implications for future learning. You could take this further by reflecting on the role play in your journal.

Online reflection

Rafferty and Steyaert (2007) explore the fact that we live in a digital society which has significantly changed the information landscape, affecting every aspect of our lives. The current wave of technological innovation is part of the context in which social work students, practitioners, and service users and carers operate. What follows are some basic ideas about this.

A blog can be used by students to write reflectively about their learning experiences and can provide a continuous record of a student's activities, progress and development.

A blog is an abbreviation of 'web log' and is designed as a web space that can be written to, published and viewed online. Blogs can be written about a wide variety of subjects and can also include audio (podcasting), video (vlog), photos (photoblog), as well as mobile blogs via a PDA (Personal Digital Assistant).

The online blog is purely a tool which enables people to publish directly to a web space which is usually personal but it could also be set up as a group space if preferred. Typically, users register with a blog and then, as they log in, their passwords identify them to the blog. Users will be able to view their most recent entry to their blogs first and older entries are archived.

Blogs can be set up using commercially available spaces that use a hosting website, for example Blogger.com, or a restricted website where users have to be pre-registered, such as a university blog. Blogs can also be customised to meet the requirements of users, for example blog entries might automatically trigger emails to supporting tutors to inform them that a new log entry has been published.

The advantage of writing reflectively online means that students can access their online logs or journals from any computer with internet access. If permissions are set up, students may choose to publish their reflective blogs to tutors, peers or to a worldwide audience.

Reflective blog entries can be structured to provide responses to set questions or left more open. Tutors or peers can provide formative feedback to blog entries that students can then respond back to and set goals for their future learning. The blog can eventually form part or all of a summative assessment, providing evidence of learning achievements.

ACTIVITY **2.6**

Search the web and read some online blogs where people have reflected upon their learning. Look at how people reflect upon their learning and the style of language they use.

Register for your own online blog (for example at Blogger.com) or your university blog and post up your next learning reflections to your blog. If desired, email the web address to your tutor or peer and ask for some constructive feedback.

Comment

The exercise should provide good insight into the variety of ways blogs can be presented, and you should also recognise that the language used is often less formal. When writing a blog, remember that the last entry is always viewed first.

Peer feedback can be extremely beneficial, and without involving the tutor it can be seen as less threatening by participants. Interestingly, peers who provide feedback can also learn through participation in the process to appreciate the value of creating constructive criticism, enabling students to become more critical and perceptive about their own learning (McConnell, 2006).

A final point about writing reflectively, particularly in journals and blogs, is that it is different from academic writing in the essential sense that it is written in the first person and not the third person. This may cause some students initial problems as they will have been encouraged in other writing to adhere to academic conventions. Writing about Open University students, Rai (2006) notes that expectations for reflective journal writing seemed to contradict the usual academic conventions. She concludes that guidance for reflective writing such as journals needs to be made explicit so that students are clear about the alternative conventions for reflective writing, such as writing in the first person about the self, about feelings and about skill development, whether this is for learning and/or assessment. We would encourage you to carefully share your learning using social networking as part of your ongoing professional development.

Skills laboratory work

Used sensitively and competently, skills laboratory work can greatly enhance student reflection on their performance, particularly in communication and interview skills. The students undertake interview-type scenarios and are filmed doing so. These scenarios can either be previously prepared or they can arise from the students' own practice situations, such as might have been selected for presentation of a critical incident for analysis. Thus a more visual form of reflection is encouraged.

The resulting feedback acts as a *mirror*, as outlined in Chapter 1. You may find that having your skills recorded for analysis is a frightening experience to begin with but eventually you will come to appreciate the learning that can be achieved by this form of reflection and analysis. Learning to give feedback to fellow students is a good skill to learn, as it is an important social work skill. The use of audio/visual recording methods helps to provide evidence to support the feedback. It also allows the student to reflect on the skills they have demonstrated in the recording and be given guidance either from fellow students or tutors on how they can enhance their performance in future. The aim of all feedback is to encourage reflection on practice and provide ideas for improvement of performance.

ACTIVITY 2.7

The importance of feedback in the reflective process cannot be overestimated, so work in pairs on the following tasks:

- *Share with your partner some verbal or written feedback that you have recently been given about your skills, either from a skills laboratory workshop or from a practice educator's observation of practice.*

- *Share how you responded to the feedback. For example, were the comments unexpected, and did you agree or disagree with them? What feelings were raised for you from the feedback?*

- *What steps you will take to improve your performance?*

- *Your partner should give their response to what has been shared, including comments on any anti-oppressive issues.*

Exchange roles and repeat the exercise.

Comment

This exercise requires good listening skills, trust, respect and courage to share in a supportive space and to receive honest feedback. Try not to become complicit with your partner but to give praise where appropriate and also ideas for improvement, such as helpful resources including readings, web pages, people who might help, etc.

John was very anxious about being filmed in the skills laboratory and did all he could to avoid the experience. Eventually, however, he was encouraged to take part in a listening exercise in the laboratory. In spite of being nervous, the feedback he received from both students and staff was very encouraging. They told him that he appeared calm and confident, he made good eye contact, his body language clearly showed that he was listening and his responses were thoughtful. He also learned that his voice was very quiet and he needed to develop his tone of voice and volume.

Non-verbal techniques

Much of what we have written in this chapter has been about verbal and written approaches to getting started in reflection. However, here are a number of non-verbal techniques that some students may find helpful in getting started. Others may find them less helpful. Some can be integrated with the verbal and written approaches.

Many students find these approaches to reflection both challenging and fun. They can be also used with service users for whom written and verbal approaches are difficult. Generally they come under what is termed 'right-brain activities', as follows:

- using aesthetic approaches such as drawing, sculpting, making collages, making or listening to music, composing a poem;
- graphical exercises such as drawing life lines or route maps;
- projective techniques such as photographs, pictures, film clips, audio clips;
- relaxation with guided fantasies;
- drama, including forum theatre techniques, role plays and simulations;
- concept mapping and organograms;
- using metaphor.

ACTIVITY **2.8**

Draw, paint, or make a collage from old magazines a metaphor for your own entry into social work. This can be done either with a partner or in a small group.

Comment

Using different materials and approaches can release energy and encourage reflection in different ways. It can provide opportunity for fun and creativity and provide further insight into the process of reflection and the ways in which other students learn and develop.

Asking good questions

By making this a short separate section in this chapter we are emphasising the point that to be asked a good question either as a student or as a service user can be life-enhancing and may promote deeper reflection. You will probably spend some time on your course developing good communication skills, and asking good questions is definitely worth the effort. Unfortunately in social work practice many questions are bureaucratically designed in the form of assessment forms and questionnaires. Nevertheless, the ability to ask and be asked good questions enables deep reflection to take place. When we are asked a good question it seems to demand a thoughtful answer. Freud (1988, p110) says that asking good questions could have a liberating effect. She views good questions as gifts rather than intrusive assaults.

It is how a question is asked as well as what is asked that can make a good question. Open questions, such as those using the 5WH formula, are helpful. Who, What, When, Where, Why and How questions tend to suit thinkers who like to work in a logical, ordered or controlled way and appreciate some external direction. This is good to begin but then it may be advisable to move on fairly quickly to open reflection, to go with the flow, let go, and be relatively unstructured, promoting free writing and thinking.

ACTIVITY **2.9**

What is the best question that you have been asked on your social work course? Why was it a good question? Have you asked the same question of other people? What was the response?

Comment

We hope that the answer to this activity is that you have been asked good questions and that they made you stop and think. According to Freud (1988), asking real questions means that you stand a chance of getting real answers, which may be upsetting, painful or disturbing, so you need to be able to bear the answers.

Critical incident analysis

The process of using critical incident analysis with social work students has been used for many years (Crisp et al., 2005) and has been endorsed by the College of Social Work in the Professional Capabilities Framework. Tutor groups meeting on a weekly or bi-weekly basis, during recall days from assessed practice placements, may ask students to present to the group an analysis of an incident from their practice placement. Some students find the term 'critical' difficult to begin with, assuming that it means something negative. This is certainly not the case, as seen below. The presentation usually includes the following:

- a brief description of the incident;

- an exploration of why the incident had a particular impact on you: what made it critical;

- an examination of which theoretical concepts informed your response and intervention;

- reflection on what has been learned from the incident and how it might inform future practice.

With the presentation, which is assessed, students submit a brief report of the incident. Following feedback on both the presentation and the report the student is then required to submit a longer evaluation of the critical incident, also for assessment. This takes the learning from the incident further and places it in a broader social context, exploring issues of discrimination, inequality and oppression.

So what constitutes a critical incident? Our view is that it must be an incident that relates to an aspect of the student's own practice, and it is their own actions in response to the incident that are reflected upon. It cannot be an incident in which they were an observer, however interesting that might be. A critical incident is one that causes us to think and reflect, which leads to learning about ourselves and others (individual and organisations) or about processes. Most incidents are not at all dramatic or obvious but commonplace events that occur routinely in social work education and/or professional practice. They may include any of the following situations:

- when you felt you had done something well;

- when you had made the wrong decision;

- when something went better than expected;

- when you lacked confidence;

- when you made a mistake;

- when you really enjoyed working with someone or a group;

- when you had a feeling of pressure;

- when you found it difficult to accept or value a service user(s);

- when you felt unsupported;

- when you were worried about a service user(s);

- when you took a risk and it paid/didn't pay off.

ACTIVITY **2.10**

Select an incident from your practice and use the above framework to reflect on and analyse the incident. This is a useful exercise to complete in pairs in the first instance.

Comment

What sort of incident did you select for analysis? Was it dramatic or commonplace? It is important that you are aware that the term 'critical' does not necessarily mean dramatic or negative.

It is very likely that you will be asked to undertake something similar to this on your course, with the analysis of the critical incident being used for either formative or summative assessment. For most students, completing these in groups is an important element of learning from reflection (reflection-on-action), our own and that of others.

Narrative analysis

As suggested in Chapter 1, social work practice is often complex and messy and reflections on practice frequently endorse this. It is important therefore to try and reflect on your reflections, and this we are calling narrative analysis. This is probably a section of the chapter that may be more relevant for post-qualifying students, especially those who are training to become practice educators and/or supervisors.

Many of us find meaning in our lives from the stories or narratives that we ourselves tell or hear about ourselves, our families and friends, etc. Story is taken to mean the actual events, while narrative is the recounting of the story. Taylor (2006, p193) says that we grasp our lives in narrative – it enables us to make sense, to pattern the events of our lives. She adopts a dialogical approach to narrative, involving a narrator and an audience, attending to the interactive/performance aspects of narrative rather than its formal properties. She goes on to make the important point that in social work education reflective accounts in the form of journals, diaries, etc. tend to be taken as 'what really happened' in any situation, whereas it should be recognised that narrators select, order and report events in particular ways for particular effects. This may be particularly the case when reflective accounts or commentaries are being assessed. Students will try and structure their journals to meet the requirements for a pass grade, and write what they think the marker wants to read. In Taylor's analysis they are performing two closely connected identities, one as the competent and caring professional and the other as competent reflector, forming a composite identity as the 'reflective practitioner' (Taylor, 2006, p195). Of course, this is what this book is attempting to promote and so are social work courses that value the reflective approach, but it needs to be authentic and genuine and not 'just for the sake of'.

The aim of a narrative is to persuade the listener or reader that the story is true and that the author is to be believed. It is important that in telling the story we trust what the narrator is telling us. Both the narrator and the story need to ring true. Sometimes what helps in narration is the inclusion of actual dialogue, as this aids authenticity. In persuading the listener/reader of the veracity of the story, the inclusion of reflections on practice will help so that the narrative is not just a descriptive account but something that promotes deeper learning about the professional identity of the social worker and their view of the world of the service user. Students writing narratives and staff responsible for their assessment need to bear this in mind as they undertake their respective difficult and responsible tasks. A case could be made that such narratives should not be used for assessment but rather for formative development. We consider that assessment is part of learning and that sensitive assessment, carefully carried out and moderated, is worth the time and effort.

ACTIVITY **2.11**

Reflect back on all the activities that we have asked you to do in this chapter and in pairs identify themes/patterns that have emerged from your narratives and share them with your partner. Alternatively, if you are in placement or post-qualifying, reflect on a story that you have been told by a service user or carer for its authenticity and veracity.

Comment

This kind of reflection draws upon many of the skills already mentioned in this chapter such as observation and critical incident analysis. It is a profound part of your development as a professional.

CHAPTER SUMMARY

In this chapter we have introduced you to a number of ways of getting started in reflecting on your practice and learning how to learn. All the activities are practical and each one builds on the previous activities, helping you to develop your reflective skills. We have set the scene for you about how adults learn and why reflective practice is worth the effort. We have also discussed a wide range of ways in which your reflections will be central to your learning and practice as a social worker. Some of the ideas we have presented will appeal more than others and this itself is worthy of reflection, but we hope that you will enjoy getting started and learning more about yourself as a reflective practitioner. It is important to know what works for you and what you need to develop.

FURTHER READING

The following three books provide a good general overview of the practical skills of reflection, theory and its application to social work practice.

Cottrell, S (2003) *Skills for success: The personal development planning guide*. Basingstoke: Palgrave Macmillan.

Moon, J A (1999) *Reflection in learning and professional development: Theory and practice*. London: Kogan Page.

Thompson, N (2009) *Understanding social work: Preparing for practice*, 3rd edition. Basingstoke: Palgrave Macmillan.

Adams, K (1990) *Journal to the self*. New York: Grand Central Publishing.

Boud, D, Hough, R and Walker, D (eds) (1985) *Reflection: Turning experience into learning*. London: Kogan Page.

Boyd, E and Fales, A (1983) Reflective learning: key to learning from experience. *Journal of Human Psychology*, 23(2): 94–117.

Cottrell, S (2003) *Skills for success: The personal development planning guide*. Basingstoke: Palgrave Macmillan.

Crisp, BR, Lister, PG and Dutton, K (2005) *Integrated assessment*. Glasgow: Scottish Institute for Excellence in Social Work Education.

Freud, S (1988) *My three mothers and other passions*. New York: New York University Press.

Honey, P and Mumford, A (2006) *The learning styles questionnaire, 80-item version*. Maidenhead: Peter Honey Publications.

Kolb, DA (1984) *Experiential learning*. London: Prentice Hall.

McConnell, D (2006) *E-learning groups and communities*. Maidenhead: McGraw-Hill.

Moon, JA (1999) *Reflection in learning and professional development: Theory and practice*. London: Kogan Page.

Progoff, I (1975) *At a journal workshop: The basic text and guide for using the intensive journal*. New York: Dialogue House.

Rafferty, J and Steyaert, J (2007) Social work in a digital society. In M Lymbery and K Postle (eds), *Social work: A companion to learning*. London: Sage.

Rai, L (2006) Owning (up to) reflective writing in social work education. *Social Work Education*, 25(8): 785–97.

Taylor, C (2006) Narrating significant experience: reflective accounts and the production of (self) knowledge. *British Journal of Social Work*, 38: 189–206.

Thompson, N (2009) *Understanding social work: Preparing for practice*, 3rd edition. Basingstoke: Palgrave Macmillan.

Chapter 3

Reflecting on emotion in social work

Gill Butler

ACTIVITY 3.1

Before you read this chapter, look at the following popular sayings and quotations, then consider which most accurately reflects your views.

Nothing disturbs feeling ... so much as thinking: emotion remains the other side of reason.

(Giddens, 1992, p200)

Never let your emotions cloud your judgment.

Emotions are sometimes unavoidable.

(Observer newspaper 22.11.15)

Thinking devoid of emotional knowledge is as problematic as emotion devoid of thought.

(Morrison, 2007, p256)

Comment

These quotations raise some of the critical issues that this chapter will help you to consider. The first two typify comments that juxtapose emotion and reason. Society and the organisations that we work in are informed by this way of thinking: we need to consider what impact this has on us personally and on our social work practice. The third, taken from a debate about whether it was acceptable for journalists and judges to display their emotions, recognises the existence of emotion, but sees it as a personal issue that needs to be managed, rather than as something that may make a contribution to our understanding. Lastly, the quotation from Morrison reflects the perspective that will be argued for within this chapter, that emotions are not something that can be set aside in the interests of greater efficiency and professionalism, but rather that they are a crucial source of information, both about ourselves and others. Understanding and working with feelings and emotions is essential if we are to make sense of the complicated, sometimes frightening, emotionally charged situations that social workers are faced with.

Introduction

We will begin this chapter by drawing on the growing field of neurobiology to gain an understanding of why emotions exist, where they come from and why they are important. This increased understanding of the way in which the brain works requires a fundamental reappraisal of prevalent thinking about the contribution of emotions within society, which is of particular relevance for professional social work practice. We will then consider the way in which this challenges prevailing views of emotion, as the antithesis of reason. The impact of such thinking on social work practice will then be explored by considering some of the difficulties associated with the language of social work, which is heavily influenced by managerialism. As Munro (2011b) recognises, this cloaks the reality of social work practice in which the need to be able to understand and process our own and others' emotions is central to many of the interactions that take place. As we will see, the absence of such an understanding may be associated with notable failures in social work, where workers have been unable to think about the significance of the emotional dimension, so have been unable to recognise what was happening. The ability to recognise, name and process emotions will enable you to express yourself more effectively, so improving your practice and increasing your emotional resilience. Structured approached to reflection and the development of emotional intelligence are explored as helpful ways forward.

By the end of this chapter you will have an increased understanding of:

- the nature and purpose of emotion;

- the significance of language in constructing social work practice;

- the impact of emotion on social work practice;

- the concept of emotional intelligence;

- your own and others' emotional responses;

- the role of reflection in developing emotionally intelligent practice;

- emotion as a source of information.

Defining emotion

RESEARCH SUMMARY

Emotions were once thought to come from a particular part of the brain, but it is now recognised that they can be found throughout the entire brain (Siegel, 2015, p147). As they engage all aspects of the brain, they have the power to disrupt thought (McLannahan, 2004). Hence, if you try to read this chapter when you are upset, worried or exhausted, you may read the words in front of you, but struggle to think about their meaning, as your ability to think is disrupted by your feelings. They begin as changes in the flows of energy throughout the brain and the body, causing changes in our state of integration. We may not be conscious of this changed state, but it has an important function in readying us for action, telling us that we need to pay attention and be alert. We may feel unsettled in a way that we cannot define. Siegel (2015) explains that the value system of the brain then appraises this information (a process involving cognition) so that we decide what the stimulus means: it is it good or bad, is it safe, or a threat? This may be accompanied by physiological responses which may arise rapidly in response to certain stimuli, but may only last a short time in the absence of the trigger (when he leaves the room your anger subsides). If we reflect we are usually able to identify the trigger.

Next there is a process of differentiation, as identifiable emotions, often referred to as feelings, emerge from the altered state of mind. While there is some debate about how many basic emotions there are, most would include happiness/joy, sadness, anger, fear, surprise, anticipation and disgust. Other emotions such as envy, shame and gratitude may be seen as stemming from or arising from various combinations of these. Feelings are usually conscious and have an object – for example, a person who has made you angry.

They are also therefore part of the process of making judgements (he has made you angry because you are upset by his treatment of his partner) and so reveal our values. Howe (2013, p48) explains that There are complex links and information sharing taking place between many areas of the brain. He summarises research by Eisenburg and Eggum, explaining that the brain responds rapidly and intuitively to information received through emotions, but more slowly to information received by the thinking 'rational' cortical area of the brain.

Moods do not usually have an object; they are less intense, longer-lasting affective states that may affect the way we view things. Often we may be unclear about what has caused the mood. As they are more muted than emotions, they may have a less immediate impact on our responses, but may still affect our perceptions and judgement.

The purpose of emotion

Emotions can serve an important purpose in alerting us to the potential need to alter our goals. Originally this may have been to ensure survival, hence the importance of very rapid emotional responses designed to ensure safety (McLannahan, 2004). Porges (2009) has developed a theory that in addition to the primitive, *reactive* fight, flight or freeze responses to threats, there is a more highly evolved way of ensuring safety, namely a *receptive* emotional response, that activates the *social engagement system.* He suggests that this is the one that we generally use: if we can see someone is becoming annoyed, we may first try to calm their anger or apologise. If this does not work we may then resort to the fight or flight response. If the social engagement response works, the flow of energy giving rise to the emotion subsides, allowing us to return to a state of integration. Sometimes we call these responses gut feelings or instinct.

Comment

As social workers, it is important to recognise the function of our emotions in alerting us to situations that we may need to pay attention to. Emotion can provide us with access to information about ourselves and about others, which we may otherwise not be conscious of. With careful reflection we may be able to process what we are feeling, making conscious use of it, in order to understand and manage our responses and to gain greater insight into the lives of those we are working with.

Emotions and rationality

From the time of Greek philosophers such as Plato until the present day, reason has dominated the development of Western philosophical thinking as the basis for determining what is good (Turner and Stets, 2005; Hugman, 2005). This creates particular difficulties in relation to recognising the contribution of emotion to understanding, which are compounded by thinking in a way that is described as *dualistic* (Bock and James, 1992). By that we mean that we think in terms of either/or, for example black or white, good or bad. We also tend to think in terms of one state being preferable to the other; this is known as *asymmetric dualism*. The positive qualities of one imply that the other is negative, or less desirable. This way of thinking can unconsciously limit our ability to appreciate difference. As a result, rather than seeing emotion as part of cognition and logical thought, it is defined in opposition to reason, as unreliable and subjective (Hugman, 2005, p48). Williams and Bendelow (1998) argue that as part of this tradition, reason has been associated with masculinity and public life, whereas emotion has been associated with women and relegated to private life. Hence, working with emotions is an area that has been largely invisible, undertaken primarily by women and conflated with notions of women's 'natural' caring role (Smethurst, 2004).

Feeling rules

While emotions arise within the mind and body from a response to stimuli, our feelings are expressed within specific cultural contexts that convey expectations about what people are supposed to feel in particular situations. These are known as *feeling rules* (Garey et al., 2011). So, for example, it may be expected that people who are attending a funeral will look sad, but that open displays of crying and grief will be limited to close friends and family. Cultural expectations about how men and women should behave may be different, putting particular pressure on those who do not conform to the expected norms of behaviour. In some cultures in the East the *feeling rules* require that any expression of negative emotions such as frustration or irritation are avoided.

ACTIVITY **3.2**

Can you identify the feeling rules in your current or last workplace?

How did these expectations affect you?

How did they affect the service users with whom you work?

What happened if people did not conform to these expectations?

Comment

We may feel embarrassed by talking about our feelings, particularly at work, as we may think that expression of emotion should be confined to our private lives, or we may worry that we may be seen as irrational. At a personal, professional and organisational level the unspoken rules and expectations about the role of emotion within professional life will vary, so in some contexts, it may be permissible to talk about feelings, while in others it may be far more difficult.

Ingram (2015) argues for the importance of recognising that place of emotion within professional practice. He conducted research with social work practitioners that explored their views about emotion and their practice. This highlighted a reluctance to record or write about their feelings and variability in their experience of feeling safe to express their emotions, particularly within the context of supervision. Interestingly this research does not consider whether gender impacts on attitudes towards working with and expressing emotion. While there may be some changes in relation to gendered expectations about the expression of feelings, the impact of these arguably still needs careful consideration, as illustrated by recent research into men's suicides. In 2014, 4,623 men committed suicide, and this figure constituted 76 per cent of all suicides in that year (Campaign Against Living Miserably, CALM). Of 2,000 men interviewed for the survey commissioned by CALM, 43 per cent said that they did not seek help because they did not want to talk about their feelings or felt ashamed, and 49 per cent said that they did not want to worry people. Issues relating to gender thus continue to need attention, and will be discussed further in Chapter 7.

What does the language of social work tell us about the construction of social work practice?

Until relatively recently little attention has been paid to the significance of language as both reflecting and shaping notions of effective social work practice (Gregory and Holloway, 2005). However, through writing and talking, practitioners and academics demonstrate what they are preoccupied with and believe to be important. The language used in legislation, policy and management has the power to shape practice in a top-down way, whereas the user and carer movements have exerted power from the bottom up by challenging the labels applied to them by professionals. This is discussed further in Chapter 5. The changing nature of social work and attitudes towards emotion are thus revealed through the language that is used.

A historical perspective

Gregory and Holloway (2005) outline stages in the development of social work. They describe the initial phase as a moral enterprise. Its roots came from the work of the social reformers at the end of the nineteenth century, who endeavoured to reform the morals of those who, as a result of their moral weakness, lived in impoverished circumstances, regardless of how they might feel about this! A good example of the language which reflects their concerns can be found in this list from the NSPCC in 1901, which identifies the following child-abusing types:

the devil-may-care and idler

the drunkard

the married and unfaithful

the married and estranged

the unmarried

the tramp

the better and gambler

the speculator in child life insurance

the avaricious and greedy.

This reformist approach broadly persisted until the 1950s when therapeutic psycho-social approaches gained in popularity. Here the aim was to treat people, who were defined as clients, with a focus on the individual and interpersonal relationships. The work of Biestek (1961) was highly influential. He identified seven principles which he considered essential to effective practice. Of these the first two focus directly on the emotional component of practice and the other five also pay attention to the nature of the 'client/worker' relationship:

- purposeful expression of feelings
- controlled emotional involvement
- individualisation
- acceptance
- non-judgemental attitude
- client self-determination
- confidentiality.

In the 1970s the Marxist analysis presented by radical social workers endeavoured to challenge the individualistic focus of therapeutic social work, locating problems within the context of structural inequality, hence the focus shifted away from the quality of individual relationships. The overall aim of radical social work was to empower people to change the system that oppressed them. Bailey and Brake (1975, pp57–8) highlight the importance of:

education (development of critical consciousness)

systems linking

counter-systems building.

However, alongside this, treatment-based problem-solving approaches continued to form the basis for mainstream social work practice.

In the 1980s the language used began to shift again to focus on the tasks that were expected of social workers. Confidence in social work was at a low ebb, which opened the door for increasing bureaucratisation and the steady rise of managerialism. Language from this period reflects the emphasis on following procedures, achieving outcomes, evidence-based practice and key performance indicators as a way to address perceived failures in practice. There was an emphasis on technical proficiency and empirical data as the essential platform for competent performance of the tasks required of social workers. The limitations of this approach were demonstrated in the 2002 National Occupational Standards (NOS) for social work. Ostensibly they provided a framework for developing the competence required of a 'beginning social worker' and a model representing the holistic nature of social work practice. However, by framing this entirely in terms of values, roles and tasks, the affective or 'third dimension' of practice is invisible. There were no references to feelings, emotions or indeed reflection, but 17 references to managing. There was a similar absence of references to emotion and feeling in the subject benchmark statement.

In a climate where the defensive adherence to procedures has been seen as a vital mechanism to ensure survival and avoid the possibility of blame or criticism, it is arguably difficult for social work to maintain a focus on the significance of relationships and feelings. The Munro Review (2011b, p6) identifies the concern of social workers to *do the right thing, rather than doing things right*. In a critical political and media environment it is unsurprising that technical rationality was more attractive to an emerging profession seeking to gain status alongside established professional groups. Munro's Review was accompanied by a growing recognition within the social work profession that knowledge, skills and rational thought are insufficient to help us properly understand, nor to equip us to respond effectively, when faced with powerful emotions, such as grief, fear, anger and hostility, which can overwhelm both service users and practitioners (Ferguson, 2011; Ruch et al., 2010, Trevithick, 2014; Wilson et al., 2008).

These concerns have been accompanied by a resurgence in interest in *relationship-based practice* which builds on earlier psycho-dynamic approaches to practice, but also includes a recognition of the impact of structural issues and diversity. The language of *relationship-based practice* highlights the importance of recognising that people are not simply rational beings and that the emotions of both service users and practitioners are central to social work practice (Wilson et al., 2008).

Alongside the renewed interest in relationship-based practice, the language of the current Professional Capabilities Framework (2012) also provides a significant change of emphasis by moving away from the detailed technical prescription of the NOS. In identifying the need for social workers to develop emotional resilience in order to manage the emotional impact of practice, there is an explicit recognition that social work is often an emotionally charged activity. Thus, within the profession there is a readiness to consider the implications of increased understandings of the working of the brain and of the purpose of emotion. However, the current neo-liberal policy context provides a challenging landscape for those seeking to move away from the reductionist technical competency-based approaches of the end of the twentieth century.

The impact of emotion on practice

RESEARCH SUMMARY

There have been several important critiques of the Laming Report (2003) into the death of Victoria Climbié in 2000 (Ferguson, 2005; Foster, 2005; Rustin, 2005). While the focus is primarily on issues raised in relation to child protection, they also have wider relevance to social work practice. The inquiry carefully details the many missed opportunities to recognise the tragic circumstances of Victoria's life and highlights the failure to do the simple things properly. Resource issues, poor interprofessional communication, inexperience, failures in accountability and poor management are seen as the major reasons for the failure to protect Victoria. However, the inquiry fails to move from the relatively superficial, albeit meticulous presentation of the data to an in-depth exploration of why, on this as well as on notable previous occasions, despite working very hard, practitioners were unable to attribute meaning to what they were seeing and to recognise the deep distress of the child. This was illustrated by the comment of one social worker who had said that Victoria looked like an advert for Action Aid.

It is argued that this state of seeing but not seeing, knowing and not knowing needs to be understood from a psychoanalytic perspective. We can then begin to understand that the difficulties may be seen as defence mechanisms operating to protect the workers. If we deny what we see and what we feel, then we do not have to acknowledge the true horror of the situation, which feels unbearable. It therefore removes the need for workers to take action to protect Victoria, so protecting themselves from a potentially very frightening experience, given the power of her aunt (Ferguson, 2005). Cooper and Lousada (2005) explore the pervasiveness of these defensive mechanisms in relation to the wider development of social policy and organisational practice.

The summary above provides a helpful illustration of the difficulty for practitioners faced with deeply distressing and frightening situations, which may result in the worker being unable to act, because the feelings aroused are unbearable and therefore denied. We may dismiss our fears and anxieties as irrational feelings, to be kept private.

They may also be denied because we are not confident about the important role of feelings as an invaluable source of information, for some of the reasons outlined above. Munro provides a very clear explanation of the complexity of the sources of information that social workers need to pay attention to:

> *the conscious mind is paying attention to the purpose of the visit; at an intuitive level they are forming a picture of the child and family and sensing the dynamics in the room, noting evidence of anger, confusion, or anxiety. This feeds into their conscious awareness and shapes the way the interview progresses. Their own emotional reaction is one source of information.*

(2011a, p35)

However, possible negative impacts and risks created by the arousal of our own emotions also need to be carefully considered, as the case study below demonstrates. In this situation feelings of loss are evoked and avoided.

CASE STUDY

Vivienne is a student who came to Britain from Zimbabwe five years ago. She has audio-recorded an interview in preparation for an assignment where she will be required to analyse her communication skills. The recording is played back in the tutorial group, which provides Vivienne with an opportunity to receive feedback from the group. The interviewee was seeking asylum. When she started to speak about her sadness in relation to home and members of her family who were left behind, the student interviewer responded by asking her about her financial difficulties and benefits. When asked by her tutor why she had done this, her initial response was that she had changed the subject because she did not want to upset the interviewee.

ACTIVITY 3.3

Write down a list of feelings that the interviewee was conveying to the interviewer.

- *How might the interviewer have felt as she listened to this?*
- *Why?*
- *What effect might changing the subject have had on the interviewee?*

Comment

In the previous section we have considered some examples that demonstrate the difficulties that can arise when practitioners are unable or unwilling to recognise the feelings of others. As we have seen, we may do this in some situations to protect ourselves from those feelings and to remove the need to respond to the situation. However, it is likely that this will not only lead to us failing to recognise issues, but will also contribute to stress and burn-out. In other situations that are less threatening, we may still lack confidence and so fail to pay sufficient attention to the emotional dimension of the interaction. As a result our responses are not fully attuned to the needs of the service user and may be experienced as unhelpful or inappropriate, as in the example of Vivienne.

The absence of a language to identify the significance of the emotional component of practice exacerbates the problem. If, as suggested earlier, emotion is contrasted with reason, we may not recognise the value of exploring the emotional component of practice, paying close attention to the affective elements of communication and systematically analysing feelings.

In the next sections we will attempt to address these difficulties by exploring the language of feelings and emotions in more depth and considering their role. We will then draw on the work of Solway developed by Goleman (1996) and constructs from psychoanalytic theory to help us to understand and work with feelings and emotions more effectively.

Talking about emotion and feelings

In the first moments that we experience an emotion, any attempt at expressing it verbally may seem impossible. As we start to appraise the emotion and it emerges as a conscious feeling, we can then try to find words that express it. While there are hundreds of words that we can use to discuss emotion, in practice our vocabularies tend to be restricted. The following activity is designed to help you to develop greater fluency in the language of emotion.

ACTIVITY 3.4

This activity would be best completed with a partner.

1. Write down a list of as many words to describe feelings that you can think of.

- *Underline the feeling words that you use regularly.*
- *Share this list with your partner. Notice similarities and differences. Explore possible reasons for this (for example, culture, gender, age).*

2. Make another list of the emotions that you have felt in the last two days.

- *Try to identify the triggers that caused you to feel these emotions.*
- *Identify what you were doing at the time when you felt each emotion.*
- *Consider the strength of the emotional responses that you have listed. Were they mild, moderate or intense?*

3. How far do you consider that your feelings conformed to expectations about what was appropriate?

Comment

Our fluency in identifying, expressing and evaluating feelings will have an impact on our ability to process them and therefore to develop resilience, as well as enhancing our ability to support others in expressing their feelings.

Putting emotions to work

We now know that in order to make sense of a situation, activity across the whole brain is required. We need to identify and reflect on how we feel as our emotions may add a crucial dimension to our understanding. As Munro (2011a), drawing on the work of Hammond, explains, we *need to see logical and intuitive thinking on a cognitive continuum* (p37). We also know that emotion is closely linked to motivation, so what we feel will influence our actions. You may know that you need to have written 1,000 words by the end of the day in order to have your essay completed on time, but if you feel upset by something you may be unable to motivate yourself to do this, although rationally you know that you should. However, if you associate completing essays on time with previous experiences of success (you got 80 per cent last time!), you are more likely to be able to motivate yourself to persevere than if your previous experiences were of failure.

A good understanding of the relationship between emotion, cognition and actions will enable us to harness our emotions in order to act more appropriately and achieve our goals.

CASE STUDY

It is Friday afternoon and I am planning to make sure my case records are up to date, as I will not be in until Wednesday next week.

I have been working with a woman who is thought to have some degree of learning difficulty. She is pregnant and is the mother of two small children. They were referred to social services by the health visitor, who has concerns about her ability to cope with a third child and about the developmental progress of the children. She says that the mother avoids contact and is dismissive. The case is seen as low priority (Children Act 1989 section 17) and appropriate for a student.

Over the last fortnight during the course of two visits she tells me that her partner does not think this third baby is his. On the second occasion she was tearful and mentions that her partner came home the other night rather the worse for wear. She hesitates, then assures me he is very good with his kids and that she can cope without any help. The children are appropriately dressed and have some toys. They are very quiet and seem undemanding and rather subdued.

ACTIVITY 3.5

Working in pairs, identify a situation where you have not done what you think you should have done.

Take a sheet of paper and write three headings: Intended action, What I actually did, Feelings at the time. *Complete the columns with reference to the situation that you have identified. An example of what this might look like in relation to the situation described above is provided in Figure 3.1.*

(Continued)

Intended action	What I actually did	Feelings at the time
Write up case notes from the visits in order to discuss them with my manager next week.	Had a cup of tea, chatted to a colleague about plans for the weekend; made some phone calls to set up some non-urgent visits.	Unsettled. Rather low. Worried, but not sure about what.

Figure 3.1

Discuss with your partner the relationship between your thoughts about what you plan to do, your feelings and your actions.

Consider how ___ *help/hinder you if you are more aware of the relationship between your thoughts,* ___ *nd feelings.*

Could you use thi ___ *upervision?*

Emotion and critical thinking

There is increasing recognition of the role of emotion in critical thinking and deep learning. Moon (2005) identifies an approach that *includes emotional as well as cognitive and whole person functioning* (p7). Clearly the ability to think critically is essential for social workers, but the importance of emotion in this process is not always recognised. Sometimes there is a mistaken belief that we must just concentrate on the facts.

RESEARCH SUMMARY

Ruch (2005) found in her research that it was possible to categorise reflective practitioners into two broad groupings of technical or holistically oriented practitioners. She found that the former tended to concentrate on practical issues and were principally concerned with reviewing what had happened and how it had happened in order to improve their practice. The holistic practitioners included these aspects of reflection, but in addition considered why things had or had not happened. She found that the holistic practitioners paid greater attention to emotional processes and were more aware of the importance of self-awareness. This facilitated responsive, relationship-based approaches to practice. As a result they were also more able to tolerate uncertainty and risk.

Developing emotional intelligence

The concept of emotional intelligence is based on a recognition of the crucial role of emotion in shaping cognitive thought and determining what we do. The emotionally intelligent person is thus able to sense, understand and use emotions in order to improve their own effectiveness and their relationships with others (www.6seconds.org). While there are mixed views about the nature of emotional intelligence, the value of some of the work on emotional intelligence and the claims made in relation to its success in improving effectiveness, it can provide a helpful framework for developing emotional literacy. This involves being able to recognise what you are feeling so that it informs your understanding and enables you to act appropriately. Such a definition suggests that emotional literacy could be key in helping practitioners in the emotional minefields of practice, where the ability to be able to accurately identify our own feelings and those of others in order to be able to act appropriately is crucial, as identified in the case of Victoria Climbié. The relevance and value of emotional intelligence in social work practice is confirmed by Ingram (2013, p994), who has demonstrated that there are very close links between what service users want from practitioners, the core values of social work and the key elements of emotional intelligence.

Self-awareness

Goleman's (1998) work on emotional intelligence recognises emotional self-awareness as an essential first stage of using emotion effectively. He draws a distinction between characteristics of emotional competence in relation to self, which is referred to as personal competence, and in relation to interactions with others, social competence. The model then moves on to provide a framework which suggests that as we develop greater awareness, we can begin to regulate our behaviour in order to be more effective, both personally and socially, as summarised in Figure 3.2.

The reflective activities suggested earlier in this chapter are designed to help with the first stage of emotionally competent practice, by developing your ability to

	Self: Personal competence	Other: Social competence
1. Awareness 2. Regulation/Action	Self-awareness	Social awareness
	Emotional self-awareness	Empathy
	Accurate self-assessment	Service orientation
	Self-confidence	Organisational awareness
	Self-control	Attuned responses
	Ability to soothe ourselves	Effective communication
	Ability to delay gratification	Ability to manage conflict
	Conscientiousness	Provide leadership
	Adaptability	Change catalyst
	Achievement	Collaborative
	Drive	
	Initiative	

Figure 3.2

(Adapted from www.eiconsortium.org with permission)

53

notice and then to accurately identify an expanded range of emotions. Through conscious reflection we can develop our awareness of our feelings and what has triggered them. We can then start to focus on the feelings of others, noticing and reflecting on their meaning. One way of doing this is by exploring our responses to particular triggers in small groups. Visual stimuli such as photographs or excerpts from television programmes, documentaries and films can be used for this purpose as they encourage emotionally direct writing. It may also be useful to consciously imagine how characters feel, a technique that Howe (2013, p172) identifies and that has been used to help aggressors to develop empathy with victims. The following activity combines this approach with the technique of guided reflection using a framework of *cue questions* (Wilson et al., 2008, p22).

ACTIVITY 3.6

Work with a partner or in small groups.

Watch a five to ten minute extract from a film or television programme (programmes such as Super Nanny *available on YouTube provide useful material). Do not take any notes, just observe. Afterwards write down:*

- *what you saw – do this as a free-flowing narrative;*

- *what you felt when you were watching it;*

- *the feelings, as you perceived them, of the actors;*

- *your feelings now as you write this up – include any other memories, thoughts or feelings that were stirred by this process and record them.*

Share your responses with your partner and discuss the similarities and differences in your observations and the feelings that this experience evoked.

Comment

This activity will help you to be more aware of your own emotional responses. It will also demonstrate how subjective your observations are. No two people will feel or see exactly the same things in any situation. Often there are different opinions and feelings about the same event. This exercise may help us to be more open-minded and less judgemental about how each of us perceives the world. Observations are influenced by our previous experience as well as by our personal identity which includes our class, gender, age, disability, ethnicity and sexuality.

Child observation

Some social work courses include the opportunity to undertake a series of observations of an infant or young child, using an adaptation of a method originally developed for training child psychoanalysts and pioneered at the Tavistock Clinic. Students are asked to write up their observations in a similar way to that suggested above and then to present them to a small seminar group. This can be a helpful way of developing our self-awareness, particularly in relation to understanding where feelings may be coming from, as memories of our own previous experiences of being parented and/or parenting are often stirred by this process. Trowell and Miles suggest that:

> social workers need to be capable of taking an observational stance to give themselves the possibility of objectivity in coming to their conclusions. The observational stance requires them to be aware of the environment, the verbal and non-verbal interaction; to be aware of their own responses as a source of invaluable data, provided that they are aware of what comes from them and what comes from their clients; and to develop the capacity to integrate these and give themselves time to think before arriving at a judgement or making a decision.

> (1996, p125)

The ability to use our emotional responses as a source of information may enrich our practice greatly and enable us to understand the meaning of some of the difficult and painful situations that we may be faced with. However, the need to be aware of what comes from us, and what comes from others, is critical. Good supervision is clearly essential, as is an understanding of the processes of transference and counter-transference.

Transference

Sometimes when we say something to someone we are taken aback by their response, which seems to us to have been out of all proportion or unrelated to what we have said. If we are surprised in this way, it is useful to consider whether transference may have taken place.

The concept of transference was first identified by Freud, who noticed that not only were his patients' reactions sometimes unrelated to anything that was taking place in their relationship with him, they also had fantasies about him that bore no relation to reality (Conner, 2001). From this he developed a theory that their responses might be triggered by a memory of an earlier experience, which unconsciously then determined their feelings and responses in the present relationship with him. This phenomenon is consistent with the research noted by Goleman (1998), leading to his conclusion that the emotional mind may react to the present as though it were the past. Transference reactions may be positive or negative. I may, for example, assume that someone who enjoys a particular food that reminds me of my father, of whom I have fond memories, is a kind and patient person, when in fact there is no evidence to support this assumption. Similarly, I may find myself wondering why I am finding it hard to work with someone who reminds me of someone I knew and disliked as a teenager, and happens to have the same name. Examples of transference are often found in the educational context.

CASE STUDY

Linda is a student plagued by fear of failure and feels unable to talk about this, either to her tutor, who she knows has been very supportive to other students, or in the tutor group that she has been part of for two years. This is a supportive group and other students in it often gain support from each other by sharing problems and exchanging ideas. She has obtained good results on the course so far, but believes that somehow this must just be luck, which is bound to change soon. Linda is convinced that the other members of her tutor group will make fun of her if she discusses her anxieties and that she will be exposed as being stupid. As a child she was expected by her parents to get on with things without asking for help. She was bullied at school and did poorly in her GCSE examinations. Her school teachers seemed uninterested in her.

Counter-transference

This is a related concept, where your own (repressed) feelings are unconsciously placed on the other person. If we continue with the example of Linda, her tutor starts to wonder if she has the ability to help her, and wonders if Linda will ever make any progress.

ACTIVITY 3.7

Identify an interaction on placement where you are left thinking, 'Why did they react like that?' How can you use your understanding of transference to further your understanding of interactions with service users and colleagues?

Regulation and action: emotionally intelligent practice

The reflective activities so far have helped us to notice what is happening in relation to our own feelings and those of others, so that we are more personally and socially aware, congruent and empathic. We can then move on to consider how we can use this awareness to regulate or channel our energy and act in such a way that we have harnessed the insight that we have gained. This can help us to behave in ways that are socially skilled and assist in managing emotion in our relationships with others. Again, reflection can provide a pathway to achieving this. In the next case study the social worker uses reflection to ensure that he communicates effectively and works in a collaborative rather than a confrontational way.

Dave, a social worker in a busy community learning disability team, is checking his emails. He has five minutes before he needs to leave to go to a case conference involving a service user he has been working with. He is anticipating that it will be difficult as the child care team are extremely critical of her parenting. Dave feels they have failed to provide adequate support and are patronising towards her. He opens an email from the manager of a local day centre headed URGENT. The email is personally critical and demands an immediate response from Dave as he has not completed all the details on a referral form that he recently sent through. The email further states that they will not deal with the referral until he has done so. Dave knows it will be difficult to find these details and considers that the referral needed urgent action. He notices that it has been copied to his manager. He is tempted to reply angrily, but instead prints out the email, in order to reflect before he responds. Later Dave reads the email again and (using a similar framework of cue questions to that suggested for Activity 3.6) writes down:

- *what was happening when he received the email;*
- *how he felt when he received the email;*
- *what he thought the manager might have been feeling when she sent the email;*
- *what he feels now;*
- *how he might channel his feelings to use them constructively;*
- *what actions might be helpful to ensure that his long-term goals are achieved.*

He was then able to respond appropriately to the email, recognising that they were both under pressure; his need was to ensure that a service was provided, but she needed the additional information in order to deliver an appropriate service.

It can also be helpful when reflecting to consider the impact of your feelings on your:

- *communication with others;*
- *energy levels;*
- *ability to complete routine tasks;*
- *ability to make decisions.*

Comment

The impact of emotion on the achievement of goals can be very positive, so it is useful to take time to reflect on both positive and apparently negative experiences. The particular value of writing about difficult experiences and our feelings about them has been highlighted in research studies by Pennebaker (2007) that have found that people who had been made redundant who were required to write about this on four consecutive days for 15 minutes a day were more likely to succeed in finding another job, as they were able to process their anger, achieve insight and channel their actions to achieve their new goals. In a similar study improvements were also found in people's physical well-being, as measured through their immune systems (Pennebaker, 1997). Research with trainee social workers by Grant and Kinman (2012) has found that emotional intelligence, empathy and reflective ability are important predictors of emotional resilience, hence the development of these competencies is useful not only for our practice, but also in helping to ensure our own well-being.

CHAPTER SUMMARY

Developments in neuroscience support the need to pay serious attention to emotions. Emotional activity 'pervades all mental functions' (Siegel, 2015, p184). Conscious awareness of the emotions present is needed if we are to understand the meaning of a situation. Without a careful analysis of the emotional dimension of practice, there is a risk that information is missed and reasoning is diminished. We need to see emotion and reason as complementary rather than opposing states of awareness.

Historically, however, emotion has been seen as hindering rational thought. It is perhaps therefore not surprising that as social work has struggled to gain recognition as a profession it has had a somewhat ambivalent approach to recognising the centrality of emotions to effective practice. The prevailing managerialist approaches, stressing technical competence and marginalising the importance of building and sustaining effective relationships, have been shown to be inadequate to deal with the complex situations that social workers need to deal with, where what is going on is often charged with emotions and barely within conscious understanding.

There is thus a need to be able to understand and express our own emotions – *personal competence* – and to understand and work with the emotional communication of those we are working with – *social competence*. The development of emotional intelligence through reflection on emotion may hold the key to enabling you to do this and will help you to be resilient. The reflective exercises outlined above and in Chapter 1 will help you with this. Failure to recognise this dimension of practice may at the least be seen to miss the point and at worst may result in an inability to understand the meaning of important information. It is therefore essential that your reflection includes this third dimension of reflection on emotion. The importance of good supervision in supporting this process will be discussed further in Chapter 9.

FURTHER READING

Cooper, A and Lousada, J (2005) *Borderline welfare: Feeling and fear of feeling in modern welfare.* London: Karnac.

Coming from a psychodynamic perspective the authors explore in much greater depth the significance of defence mechanisms that operate to protect society from certain forms of feeling. The impact of this on policy and practice is explored and includes an excellent analysis of the Laming report.

Goleman, D (2004) *Emotional intelligence and working with emotional intelligence.* London: Bloomsbury.

A good introduction to emotional intelligence for those who would like to explore this further.

Ingram, R (2015) *Understanding emotions in social work*. Maidenhead: Open University Press.

This new text provides a welcome and comprehensive overview of emotions in social work and draws on research with social work practitioners, undertaken by the author.

USEFUL WEBSITES

www.eiconsortium.org

Useful website with examples of research into a range of approaches to developing emotional intelligence.

REFERENCES

Bailey, R and Brake, M (eds) (1975) *Radical social work*. London: Arnold.

Biestek, F (1961) *The casework relationship*. London: Allen & Unwin.

Bock, G and James, S (1992) *Beyond equality and difference*. London: Palgrave.

CALM: www.thecalmzone.net/2015/11/why-we-need-to-discuss-men, research into male suicide. Accessed 26.11.2015.

Conner, MG (2001) Transference: are you a biological time machine? *The Source*. www.crisiscounselling.com (accessed 11.2.2007).

Cooper, A and Lousada, J (2005) *Borderline welfare: Feeling and fear of feeling in modern welfare.* London: Karnac.

Ferguson, H (2005) Working with violence, the emotions and the psycho-social dynamics of child protection: Reflections on the Victoria Climbié case. *Social Work Education*, 24(7): 781–95.

Ferguson, H (2011) *Child protection practice*. Basingstoke: Palgrave Macmillan.

Foster, A (2005) Surface and depth in the Victoria Climbié Report. *Child and Family Social Work*, 10: 1–9.

Garey, A, Hansen, K and Ehrenreich, B (2011) *At the heart of work and family: Engaging with the ideas of Arlie Hochschild.* Rutgers University Press.

Giddens, A (1992) *The Transformation of Intimacy.* Cambridge: Polity Press.

Goleman, D (1996) *Emotional intelligence*. London: Bloomsbury.

Goleman, D (1998) *Working with emotional intelligence*. London: Random House.

Grant, L and Kinman, G (2012) Enhancing wellbeing in social work students: building resilience in the next generation. *Social Work Education: The International Journal*, 31(5): 605–21.

Gregory, M and Holloway, M (2005) Language and the shaping of social work. *British Journal of Social Work*, 35(1): 37–53.

Howe, D (2013) *Empathy: What it is and why it matters*. Basingstoke: Palgrave Macmillan.

Hugman, R (2005) *New approaches to ethics in the caring professions*. Basingstoke: Palgrave.

Ingram, R (2013) Locating emotional intelligence at the heart of social work practice. *British Journal of Social Work*, 43: 987–1004.

Ingram, R (2015) *Understanding emotions in social work: Theory, practice and reflection.* Maidenhead: Open University Press.

Laming, H (2003) *The Victoria Climbié inquiry report. Cm5730*. London: The Stationery Office. Crown copyright. www.victoria-climbié-inquiry.org.uk/fine/report.pdf.

McLannahan, H (2004) *Emotions and mind 6*. Buckingham: Open University Press.

Moon, J (2005) *Critical thinking*. Bristol: Escalate.

Morrison, T (2007) Emotional intelligence, emotion and social work: context, characteristics, complications and contribution. *British Journal of Social Work*, 37: 245–63.

Munro, E (2011a) *The Munro review of child protection: Interim report: The child's journey*. Available at: www.education.gov.uk/publications/eOrderingDownload/Munro_Interim-report.pdf (accessed 24.5.2013).

Munro, E (2011b) *The Munro review of child protection: Final report – A child-centred system*. London: Department of Education. Available at: www.education.gov.uk/publications/eOrderingDownload/Munro-Review.pdf.

NSPCC (1901) *Annual Report*. NSPCC.

Pennebaker, J (1997) *Opening up: The healing power of expressing emotions*. New York: Guilford Press.

Pennebaker, J (2007) *Writing to heal: A guided journal for recovering from trauma and upheaval*. Oakland, CA: New Harbinger Publications.

Porges, SW (2009) Reciprocal influences between body and brain in the perception and expression of affect: a polyvagal perspective. In D Fosha, D Siegel and M Solomon (eds), *The healing power of emotion: Affective neuroscience, development, and clinical practice*. New York: Norton.

Ruch, G (2005) Relationship-based practice and reflective practice: holistic approaches to contemporary child care social work. *Child and Family Social Work*, 10: 111–23.

Ruch, G, Ward, A and Turney, D (2010) *Relationship-based practice: Getting to the heart of practice*. London: Jessica Kingsley.

Rustin, M (2005) Conceptual analysis of critical moments in Victoria Climbié's life. *Child and Family Social Work*, 10: 11–19.

Siegel, D (2015) *The Developing Mind*, 2nd edition. New York: Guilford Press.

Smethurst, C (2004) *Gender care and emotion work: Men in a female profession*. Unpublished MA dissertation. University of Chichester.

Trevithick, P (2014) Humanising managerialism: reclaiming emotional reasoning, intuition, the relationship, and knowledge and skills in social work. *Journal of Social Work Practice*, 28: 3.

Trowell, J and Miles, G (1996) The contribution of observation training to professional development in social work. In G Bridge and G Miles (eds), *On the outside looking in*. London: Central Council for Education and Training in Social Work.

Turner, J and Stets, J (2005) *The sociology of emotions*. New York: Cambridge University Press.

Williams, S and Bendelow, G (1998) *Emotions in social life: Critical themes and contemporary issues*. London: Routledge.

Wilson, K, Ruch, G, Lymbery, M and Cooper, A (2008) *Social work: An introduction to contemporary practice*. Harlow: Longman.

Part 2

Developing the reflective practitioner

Chapter 4

Reflection as a catalyst in the development of personal and professional effectiveness

Gill Constable

Introduction

This chapter will focus on the use of reflection to develop personal and professional effectiveness. The process of reflection will be underpinned by the development of critical thinking skills in addition to approaches derived from cognitive and behavioural theories, in particular Ellis and Dryden's (1999) ABC theory found within Rational Emotive Behaviour Therapy.

Social work is a profession with reported higher levels of stress-related ill health, such as musculoskeletal disorders, depression and anxiety, than other occupational groups

(Health and Safety Executive, 2012). It is important, then, that we do not neglect the opportunity to develop our emotional resilience, as this will impact on our attitude and behaviour towards service users and carers, as well as the quality of our life. These approaches can be shared with users and carers to help them manage stressful and difficult experiences.

The chapter will begin by giving some definitions and explanations of what is meant by reflection. An exploration will then take place into what cognitive and behavioural theories are, and how they can be applied with particular reference to patterns of thinking and behaviour that are disempowering. A number of approaches will be discussed, such as:

- defining critical thinking skills;

- writing reflectively;

- self-talk and belief systems;

- developing self-acceptance.

The chapter will follow Suzy, a student social worker, on her assessed practice placement. Suzy developed her capacity to reflect, which helped her to manage herself when working with complex and stressful situations. Suzy's progress through her placement will be structured around the framework she used in her reflective journal.

Throughout the chapter there will be several exercises for you to do that will enable you to understand how the theory and the methods arising from it can be put into use.

What do we understand by reflection?

A definition of reflection in terms of social work practice was discussed in Chapter 1. If we now return to this, Horner (2013) suggests that reflection is a prerequisite to being an effective social worker as it requires an approach that questions our thoughts, experiences and actions. This enables us to learn from experience and enhances our knowledge and skills. The important point is that through reflection as social workers we can *change* how we think, feel and behave to better meet the needs of service users and carers, as our understanding of ourselves is deepened and developed.

Where do we start?

Assessment is a fundamental process in social work and requires the development of critical thinking skills which Cottrell (2011, p2) defines as a process that incorporates:

- having the ability to recognise other people's viewpoints and their reasons for maintaining this perspective;

- being able to evaluate the evidence to support a particular view;

- having the capacity to compare and contrast different arguments;

- being able to consider issues in some depth, not just accepting superficial explanations;

- having the skill to notice when arguments are used to support a particular position that appear sound but are in fact erroneous;

- being able to reflect in a structured manner;

- having the capacity to bring together different factors and come to a conclusion;

- being able to present a well-evidenced argument that is credible to other people.

Cottrell suggests that sometimes our emotional responses can impact in an unhelpful way on our capacity to think critically. Therefore, if we learn how to recognise and manage our emotions, for example if we are aware that certain situations will affect us, we can better understand why we feel a particular way and we can learn how to manage these feelings through thinking about them critically. The experience of Josh, a student social worker, illustrates this.

CASE STUDY

As part of Josh's first practice placement he was allocated the role of link social worker with the local infant school. On his first visit it was raining heavily outside. The deputy headteacher greeted him warmly and showed him around the school. When they went through the cloakroom where all the children's wet coats hung, Josh became suddenly anxious. He felt confused about his feelings, and hoped that the deputy headteacher did not notice his discomfort. It was as if he was five years old again. Josh had been bullied by three older boys in the cloakroom, which was some distance from the classrooms. He always tried to avoid using it, but when it was raining his teacher told him to hang his coat up. It was the smell of the wet coats that brought the memory back of something that occurred 14 years earlier. Can you recall an incident when you were taken aback by a strong emotional response that you were not expecting? Did you find that understanding where these emotions came from enabled you to be more in control, even if the feelings were uncomfortable?

To assist us to reflect it can be helpful to develop a framework that we can use. In Chapter 2 a number of suggestions were made to assist the reflective process that includes creative approaches, for example the use of metaphor to describe a situation or emotion, imaginary discussions with people, events and projects, as well as working with dreams and imagery. The reflective framework that we will use will include evidence-based ideas based on facts and will also enable us to think creatively through the use of other approaches. Before we turn to a framework for a reflective journal we will consider what research suggests about the usefulness of writing to support reflection.

RESEARCH SUMMARY

Research into the positive effects of writing has been shown by Pennebaker et al. (cited by Nicolson et al., 2006 and Bolton, 2014). It could be argued that unstructured writing may lead to increased levels of anxiety if people are ruminating and dwelling on difficulties through recording them. It is therefore suggested that the template set out below is used, as this provides a process to problem solve as well as reflect on issues (Nicolson et al., 2006, p85).

Structure for a reflective journal

Stage 1: Reflect or think about an issue or concern that you have. This should be done in an unstructured manner to capture your thoughts spontaneously.

Stage 2: Analyse what you have written and ask yourself the following questions:

- What is going on here?

- What assumptions am I making?

- What does this tell me about my beliefs?

- Are there other ways of looking at this?

Be precise and specific in your analysis – paraphrase the key points. If you read your journal over a number of entries are there any themes emerging?

Stage 3: Action – answer the following questions:

- What action could I take?

- How can I learn from this?

- Would I respond differently if this occurs again?

- What does this tell me about the beliefs that I hold about myself?

To be a reflective practitioner we need to develop self-awareness and recognise how we impact on other people through our attitudes and behaviour, while being conscious of what triggers particular thoughts and emotions in us. Josh recognised that his emotional discomfort was due to an unhappy memory. Because he knew this Josh was able to manage his emotional reaction rationally. We will look at an exercise to develop self-awareness before we move on to the reflective journal template.

Developing self-awareness

There are a number of approaches that can be used to assess ourselves in terms of our personality traits and preferred learning style, which supports our self-awareness.

Strengths, Weaknesses, Opportunities and Threats (SWOT) analysis is a technique that is often used in organisations and teams to take a position statement of how the organisation or team are functioning. Nonetheless this is an extremely effective technique to use on ourselves (Thompson, 2006).

Suzy is a social work student who completed a SWOT analysis (Figure 4.1) to share with her practice educator Nasreen at her practice placement in a family centre. Suzy has been very honest in her self-analysis and shown that she has given it considerable thought. She was congratulated by Nasreen for being prepared to really look at her developmental needs, so they could develop an action plan that set out how Suzy's learning needs on the placement would be met.

Strengths	Weaknesses
I'm friendly and find it easy to get on with people. I enjoy being with children. I want to support parents to care for their children, so that their life together is happier. I am committed to working as a social worker, and motivated to learn and develop. I always work hard. I care about people and social justice.	I have a tendency to worry and experience stress (the risk of harm has been identified as a factor for most of the children I will be working with). I am unsure if I will be able to manage emotionally in this placement. I get very upset when children are not treated affectionately. I want people to like me; sometimes social workers have to make very difficult decisions, such as recommending that children be separated from their families. At times I take myself and life a bit too seriously – I need to remember to have a sense of humour!
Opportunities	Threats
To learn new skills and develop knowledge. Practise the skills and implement the theories learned on my social work course at university. Tackle my weaknesses (above) and threats (opposite)!	Find that I can't cope with the work due to being upset and getting very stressed. My fear of failure. I don't have a lot of confidence in situations of conflict. I set very high standards for myself, maybe they are not always realistic.

Figure 4.1   Suzy's SWOT analysis at the start of her placement in a family centre

---

ACTIVITY *4.1*

Do a SWOT analysis of yourself. It is important to be honest in the same way that Suzy has been. (We will return to your SWOT analysis after Activity 4.2, by which time you will have made an assessment of yourself, which you may find very illuminating.)

Comment

When tackling this exercise it will help you to use the template of four boxes. Do not try to do it in logical sequence, unless this is easiest for you. You may get more down by writing what first comes to you. You may find that what feels like a potential threat is also an opportunity, and so needs to go into both boxes.

If we continue to follow Suzy in her placement we can see how she used this self-knowledge gained from the SWOT analysis in her thoughts following an incident at the family centre which she recorded in her reflective journal. Suzy used the template that we considered earlier.

CASE STUDY

This is an example of a journal entry that Suzy took to supervision.

I was sitting with Katie (19 years old) and her daughter Amy nine months, who was on her lap. Amy spilt her drink over her and Katie.

Katie got very angry really quickly and shouted at Amy. 'You f****** dirty cow – you've messed up your new dress. Get the f**** off me.'

She then roughly put Amy on the floor. Amy started to cry and this made Katie even more angry. She told her to 'shut the f**** up'.

I watched and I froze. I was very frightened. Katie's anger was so quick. I hate myself for being frightened.

I'm pathetic, useless, weak. I can't cope. I just sat and watched.

Colleen (staff) heard the shouting and came in. She picked Amy up and gave her a cuddle, and sat near Katie. She asked Katie what had happened. Katie said that Lee (her boyfriend) has been seeing her best friend, and Amy spilling her drink was the last straw.

Colleen listened to Katie and when she had calmed down she asked Katie what effect she thought that her outburst had had on Amy. Colleen was relaxed and non-judgemental in her manner and this helped Katie to be open about her feelings and think about her behaviour.

Finally Katie took Amy from Colleen and told Amy that she was sorry that she had taken her anger out on her. Colleen discussed with Katie age-appropriate behaviour and that children do mess their clothes up. She offered to help Katie learn how to manage her frustration and angry feelings.

Following this incident I became aware that I had a headache, and my shoulders felt sore where I had tensed them. I also felt really down.

Suzy's use of the reflective journal template

When I analysed this I became aware of how I behave under stress and what I tell myself. This is a summary of the key learning points for me.

- *I froze with fear.*
- *I was frightened (although at no time did I feel threatened).*
- *I thought, 'I hate myself for not protecting or comforting Amy'.*

- *I told myself, 'I am pathetic, useless and weak'.*
- *I remember thinking, 'I can't cope'.*
- *My shoulders and neck felt sore, and I had a headache.*
- *When I now think about the incident I feel sad.*

Action

1. *To get better management of my thoughts and feelings, and to discuss with Nasreen ways that I can begin to do this.*

2. *To discuss with Nasreen offering to work jointly with Colleen to support Katie to understand Amy's needs and manage her angry feelings. (Colleen will be a good role model.)*

ACTIVITY **4.2**

Now let us return to you, and the SWOT analysis that you completed earlier.

- *What did your SWOT analysis reveal about you?*
- *What are your strengths?*
- *How might you build on them and could this impact on areas that you have identified as weaknesses?*

Comment

Start to write a reflective journal using the structure outlined above. Remember to think about actions that you could take to solve any problems or issues that you have. Try to get into the habit of doing this. You might want to take a notebook with you and jot down thoughts and observations that you have during the day, and then explore them in more detail in your reflective journal.

Action planning

In the same way that an assessment of service users or carers enables social workers to develop a care plan to meet people's needs (Parker and Bradley, 2010), so the self-assessment that Suzy has completed through the SWOT analysis, reflective journal and supervision with Nasreen heightened her self-awareness and identified specific learning needs. They identified self-management in relation to stress as one of Suzy's priorities. Together they reformulated this into a positive goal that focuses on what Suzy wants – to be personally effective in her practice – rather than emphasising what she does not want – excessive stress. This is the action plan that has been produced. Do note that part of the plan requires Suzy to use her own learning to enable service users and carers to manage stressful feelings and thoughts which may then be manifested in behaviour, as evidenced by Katie's outburst.

Suzy's action plan

Student Social Worker: Suzy Fitzgerald

Practice Educator: Nasreen Khan

Aims

- *This action plan seeks to enhance Suzy's personal effectiveness as a student social worker at Southside Family Centre.*

Objectives

- *To support Suzy to develop strategies and approaches that enable her to reduce unhelpful stress that impacts on her work within the centre, especially in relation to conflict.*
- *For Suzy to use her own self-development to support children and parents at the centre to manage stressful and unhelpful thoughts, feelings and behaviours.*
- *For Suzy to develop her capacity to take personal responsibility for her own continuous professional development and become a reflective practitioner.*

Actions

- *Suzy to write a reflective journal using the agreed structure and bring a journal extract to supervision every week for discussion.*
- *Suzy to do some research into the fight or flight theory for discussion in supervision. (This will be linked to university work.)*
- *Suzy to reflect on the use of cognitive and behavioural theories in terms of herself. (This will be linked to university work.)*
- *Nasreen to give Suzy information about breathing, neck and shoulder exercises.*
- *The learning from the above to be taught to service users and carers focusing initially on joint work between Suzy and Colleen with Katie.*

Outcomes

- *The learning that Suzy achieves in terms of the management of her own responses to stress can be used with families at the centre, many of whom experience significant stress.*

Review

- *The action plan will be discussed at supervision each week in terms of progress.*
- *A full review will take place in six weeks' time.*

The action plan requires Suzy to research into particular theories such as fight and flight, as well as learning physical exercises to manage stress. The cumulative effect of stress, over many years, has serious consequences for people's health and wellbeing.

Learning breathing exercises (Baylis cited in Linley and Joseph, 2004) has a beneficial effect on slowing the heart rate and calming the nervous system. Butler and Hope (2007) provide accessible and extensive information about relaxation exercises, as well as many other approaches to manage your emotions, thoughts and behaviour.

It is important to become aware of how you are reacting physically, so you can change your position to reduce the muscles becoming rigid. Once you do become conscious of your body the ability to reduce physical tension will enable you to feel mentally calmer. However, it is important to remember that sometimes your body may be alerting you to genuine risks.

Approaches that can help us manage our stress

As well as developing an understanding of the fight or flight theory, Suzy needs to become aware of her self-talk, and assess what this tells her about the beliefs she holds about herself. We will also consider the role that cognitive and behavioural theories can play.

If Suzy is able to integrate her understanding of these theories into her practice, it will assist her in her goal to be personally effective in her work with the families attending the family centre. Additionally she will be able to explain these approaches to the families, so together they can work on bringing about changes that will ameliorate some of the difficulties that they are experiencing.

Fight or flight theory

Goleman (1996) explains the fight or flight theory as a physiological response to situations where we believe ourselves to be in danger. Our minds think that we are about to be attacked and our bodies tense ready to either attack the perceived aggressor or run away. This response dates back to prehistoric times when human beings had to respond to many physical threats in the same way that animals do. The difficulty is that we can respond to situations in an automatic physiological manner that is disproportionate to the threat that we are experiencing.

If we return to Suzy's reflective journal, she has written:

- **I froze with fear.**

- **I was frightened (although at no time did I feel threatened).**

- **I have become aware of how often my shoulders and neck feel sore and I often get headaches.**

- **When I think about the incident I feel sad.**

In this situation Suzy's automatic physiological response was to sense danger, and she became immobilised rather like the proverbial frightened rabbit that stops in the middle of the road as a car approaches rather than run to safety. Suzy's body has tensed especially around her shoulders and neck, which has probably resulted in her getting a headache.

If Suzy had slowed her breathing, lowered her shoulders and her self-talk had been encouraging and reassuring this may have prevented her reaction.

Belief systems

Our minds are constantly full of thoughts and ideas (self-talk) which we discuss with ourselves. Sometimes our thoughts are positive and helpful while at other times they are destructive and problematic to us. The quality of our self-talk reveals what we believe about ourselves. Beliefs may or may not have any objective truth; they are quite simply what we believe to be true. In childhood we develop beliefs that are *so fundamental and deep* that we do not express them to ourselves or others (Beck, 1995, p15). Often we are not even aware of what they are. For example, children who have experienced harsh or unfair criticism about a particular behaviour may generalise this to aspects of their personality and grow up with non-affirming self-beliefs, which impact negatively on their self-esteem. If a child is told on a regular basis that they are thoughtless and ungrateful, how do you imagine this may influence their view of themselves when they reach adolescence?

Suzy's self-talk is very negative and unsupportive:

- I hate myself.
- I am pathetic, useless and weak.
- I can't cope.

If we look at these statements in more detail they suggest that Suzy is always pathetic, useless, weak and unable to cope in all situations and at all times. This is factually untrue and has impacted on her self-esteem and confidence. It has affected her mood. Suzy wrote in her reflective journal how she feels sad when she thinks about the incident with Katie and Amy.

ACTIVITY **4.3**

By starting to take notice of your thoughts you will be able to assess if your self-talk is critical and chiding like Suzy's or positive, supportive and enabling.

What do you say to yourself during times of stress? Whose voice is speaking – yours or a critical teacher or parent? Do you tell yourself 'I can't cope with one more thing to do' or 'I can do this' when the going gets tough?

Keep a record of the thoughts and images that go through your mind in your reflective journal.

Comment

Can you identify any patterns emerging? Can you relate your thoughts to changes in mood, such as suddenly feeling irritated because you have remembered a task that you have to do, or feeling excited when you think of an anticipated pleasurable event such as going on holiday?

Cognitive behaviour therapy

During the 1960s Aaron T. Beck developed cognitive behaviour therapy, which was directed towards assisting people to solve their difficulties through restructuring their thought processes. Beck trained as a psychotherapist and found that traditional psychodynamic interventions took people back to early experiences where they gained insights into the possible causes of their difficulties, but did not enable them to necessarily overcome them. Beck's developed an approach that was fixed in the present and that challenged dysfunctional thinking and behaviour.

If we consider Suzy's self-talk and how this reinforces her beliefs about herself we can see how these thoughts are problematic and in fact increase her stress, and impact on her feelings, behaviour and physiology. This can be expressed in a diagram (adapted from Beck, 1995, p18) as seen in Figure 4.2.

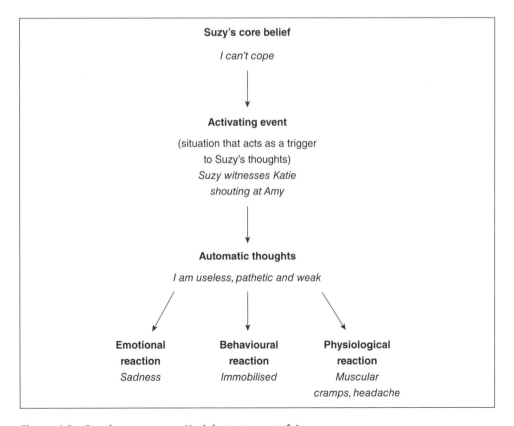

Figure 4.2   Suzy's response to Katie's treatment of Amy

Rational emotive behaviour therapy

Albert Ellis (1957) developed this therapeutic intervention which emphasises that people need to have a purpose and goals to achieve if their lives are to be satisfying. This can be undermined by irrational thoughts that prevent people achieving their goals. Ellis developed the ABC schema as a tool to challenge dysfunctional beliefs and thoughts. It operates as follows:

A = Adversity – the situation that triggered the belief

B = Belief the person holds

C = Consequence – the emotional, behavioural and physiological impact of the belief.

We often think that an event (adversity) happens and this causes us to feel or behave in a particular way. In fact it is our belief about the cause of the event that makes us feel and behave as we do. This is an example of how the approach works.

CASE STUDY

Paul has completed his BA Social Work and has applied for a vacancy in the team where he had his final placement. He is very confident that he will be offered a permanent job, as his practice educator has been very positive about his performance.

Paul contacts his personal tutor Winston at university following the interview and tells him: 'I am devastated, Winston. I didn't get the job. I don't understand. I feel really bad. It's shattered my confidence. Can I come and see you, please?'

Winston meets with Paul and they agree to structure their discussion around the ABC approach at Winston's suggestion.

Adversity – *Paul is not offered the post in the Community Mental Team where he had his last practice placement as a student.*

Consequence – *Paul explains that he feels very upset and thinks that maybe the team do not like him, and that his practice is poor.*

Winston points out that Paul has gone from the situation of not being offered the job to the consequences. In other words, Paul thinks he feels depressed because he did not get the job. In fact it is Paul's beliefs about not getting the job that has caused his depression. Winston asks him to explain what goes through his mind when he thinks about not being offered the job.

Paul says: 'I feel I am rubbish. I was OK as a student but they won't employ me. Maybe they don't like me, but I liked them. It was a great placement.'

Winston repeats back to Paul what he has said: 'I feel I am rubbish.' Winston writes down the following with Paul:

Adversity

I have not been offered a job in the team where I had my last placement.

Belief

I am rubbish.

Consequences

I feel depressed.

Winston suggests Paul should put forward arguments that dispute his self-belief that he is rubbish. Paul could do this by imagining a supportive friend is pointing out all his strengths or he has a lawyer arguing his case for him.

Disputation

Paul was able to think of the following.

- *I have achieved my BA Social Work and I am now qualified.*

- *I work hard. This can be evidenced by the tutors' comments on my dissertation.*

- *Feedback from the service users' group that I developed in my last placement about my role as the group facilitator was very positive.*

- *The manager in the hospice where I had my first placement told me that the multi-disciplinary team had so enjoyed having a social work student on placement that they would like to take another student from this university.*

Winston advises Paul that telling himself that he is rubbish was an example of negative thinking. In addition Paul had generalised about himself, blamed himself, personalised the situation and tried to mind-read the interviewing panel. For example, Paul assumed that maybe they did not like him. Winston suggested that Paul should turn negative thoughts into positive thinking habits, as he was creating for himself considerable stress by his critical and harsh attitude towards himself.

They then moved on to consider some options that Paul could pursue to learn from the experience, and plan for the future. Seligman (2002, p93) has added Energisation and Disputation to the ABC approach. This enabled Paul to set himself some tasks, and challenge his negative thinking.

(Continued)

CASE STUDY *continued*

Energisation

- *I will contact the chair of the interviewing panel and ask for feedback as to why I was not offered the job.*

- *I will take notes from this conversation and use this as a basis of an action plan. (I know that I did not sufficiently address issues about equalities in the case study, and that I could have shown more awareness about the impact of policy on local mental health services.)*

- *I will meet with the careers officer in the university and ask for some support in preparing for interviews.*

- *I will work hard on developing positive thinking habits. This is important for me personally, but also in my work with service users and carers.*

Returning to the family centre, we will see how Colleen and Suzy worked with Katie using this approach.

CASE STUDY

Katie has been attending the family centre for three weeks. During that time she has been able to discuss with Colleen and Suzy her sense of hopelessness and her expectation that Amy will be removed from her care. She has spoken about being angry with the whole world, and suspects that this is linked to the death of her mother three years ago. She knows that sometimes she speaks harshly to Amy, and then feels guilty afterwards. Using the ABC approach they worked through with Katie the incident where Amy had spilt her drink. This is set out as a conversation between Katie and Colleen (see Figure 4.3).

Adversity	Colleen	Katie, what was going through your mind before Amy spilt her drink?
	Katie	I had this picture of Lee with Sarah, who is meant to be my best friend, going out together. I thought about Mum and about how lonely I am.
Belief	Colleen	Tell me more about your lonely feelings, Katie.
	Katie	Mum was 38 when she died. I often think if she had really loved me she wouldn't have died. I know it's daft because she died of cancer. Amy's father never bothered with me and now Lee has gone.
	Colleen	Katie, are you saying that you feel unloved and no one will ever love you?
	Katie	I suppose I am.

Consequences	Katie	I get stressed out and angry about stupid things that don't matter like Amy messing her clothes up.
Disputation	Colleen	Katie, it must be hard for you to cope with the belief that you are unlovable. Even if it were true it's important that you accept yourself. Another way of thinking about this is: 'I'm my own person and I can love myself, so I will always be loved. This will make me more attractive to other people, as I will feel good about myself.'
Energisation	Colleen	Katie, do you think it would help to start to notice what goes through your mind when you are upset, or feel down? Bad moods don't just happen – there is always something that causes them. Then you can start to challenge some of those self-beliefs you have. I can show you some breathing exercises and ways of relaxing physically, as that will help too. The other thing is that we have links with the college. We could look to see if there is a course that you might be interested in. It would enable you to make new friends.
	Katie	I am already starting to think more about things. I want to be good to Amy. You are right – I have always managed on my own. I would like you to teach me how to relax. I think I've been low for so long it's got to be a habit, but I feel much better now. It helps to talk about things – you help me to see things from a different point of view.

Figure 4.3   Katie and Colleen's conversation

From Colleen's conversation with Katie we can see the impact that unfounded beliefs and negative thinking habits can have emotionally, behaviourally and physiologically for Katie and, importantly, for Amy too. For Katie and Suzy the process of reflecting and having the opportunity to talk through their insights is necessary for Katie to develop into a consistently caring parent and for Suzy as a social worker.

ACTIVITY 4.4

Think of a situation that has caused you anxiety and upset. Analyse it using the ABC approach. Reflect on your understanding of the situation now. What have you learned about your beliefs?

Comment

The ABC approach is very effective in enabling us to gain new insights into problems, and assists us to challenge ideas and beliefs that cause us difficulties. It is essential to remember that it is not the actual event that often causes us distress, but our reaction to it. If you recall, Josh became panicky when he smelt the wet coats in the cloakroom. It triggered a memory of being bullied by other children. In reality Josh was now an adult and in no danger from ever being bullied again in an infant school cloakroom.

Critique of the theory

Milner and O'Byrne (2009) state that cognitive and behavioural theories view change as required at an individual level rather than taking account of societal inequalities. In addition, the structured approach of the intervention can feel mechanistic and prescriptive, locating the difficulty in the person, rather than taking account of their social environment and experiences. Katie's situation is not understood, for example, from a feminist perspective. This would place emphasis on her as a lone parent operating within a patriarchal social system that expects her to assume care of Amy without similar requirements of Amy's father. In other words, if she had deserted Amy as her father had, this would be viewed more harshly because Katie is a woman and mother. It can of course be argued that by enabling Katie to develop the capacity of accepting herself, she will be able to dispute negative self-beliefs, which will enhance her well-being and empower her.

Being a reflective practitioner

To summarise, Suzy's development as a reflective social worker has been assisted by the following approaches that are supporting her professional and personal development.

- Through the SWOT analysis she has assessed her strengths and areas for development.

- Suzy is keeping a structured reflective journal.

- Suzy is working on developing positive thinking habits through monitoring her self-talk, developing an understanding of cognitive behaviour theory and the ABC technique.

- Suzy is co-working with an experienced member of staff (Colleen) with a view to using her as a role model to develop her own practice.

- Finally, Suzy is committed to integrating her learning into her practice, and sharing this knowledge and skills within her work with service users and carers.

These activities and approaches will be reviewed and evaluated with her practice educator, but it is important that Suzy takes personal responsibility for her own learning and development.

CHAPTER SUMMARY

In this chapter we have explored the use of self-assessment as a vehicle to start to develop reflective practice. Cognitive and behavioural theories have been the dominant theoretical perspective examined with an emphasis on its practical application for service users, carers and social workers. It is necessary to consider what approaches work for us prior to utilising them on service users and carers. Our commitment and optimism in our capacity to support people in the process of development and change lies in being able to reflect on our own beliefs, motivations and actions, and the development of positive thinking habits. If we can believe in our capacity to change and develop we can then help others to do so too.

FURTHER READING

Butler, G and Hope, T (2007) *Manage your mind*, 2nd edition. Oxford: Oxford University Press.

This is an excellent book that addresses all aspects of developing well-being, and is written in an accessible manner. It includes many helpful approaches to combating self-doubt and enhancing self-esteem.

Seligman, M (2002) *Authentic happiness*. London: Nicholas Brealey.

This book promotes the study of positive psychology rather than pathology. It provides evidence of how we can become more optimistic and positive in our outlook, thereby enhancing our own happiness and the happiness of those around us.

REFERENCES

Beck, J (1995) *Cognitive therapy basics and beyond*. New York: Guilford Press.

Bolton, G (2014) *Reflective practice, writing and professional development*, 4th edition. London: Sage.

Butler, G and Hope, T (2007) *Manage your mind*, 2nd edition. Oxford: Oxford University Press.

Cottrell, S (2011) *Critical thinking skills developing effective analysis and argument*, 2nd edition. Basingstoke: Palgrave.

Ellis, A (1957) Rational psychotherapy and individual psychology. *Journal of Individual Psychology*, 13: 38–44.

Ellis, A and Dryden, W (1999) *The practice of Rational Emotive Behaviour Therapy*. London: Free Association Books.

Goleman, D (1996) *Emotional intelligence*. London: Bloomsbury.

Health and Safety Executive (2012) *Work related research and statistics*. Available at: www.hse.gov.uk/stress/research/htm (accessed 24.5.2013).

Horner, N (2013) *What is social work? Context and perspectives*, 4th edition. Exeter: Learning Matters.

Linley, PA and Joseph, S (2004) *Positive psychology in practice*. New Jersey: Wiley.

Milner, J and O'Byrne, P (2009) *Assessment in social work*, 3rd edition. Basingstoke: Palgrave Macmillan.

Nicolson, P, Bayne, R and Owen, J (2006) *Applied psychology for social workers*, 3rd edition. Basingstoke: Palgrave Macmillan.

Parker, J and Bradley, G (2010) *Social work practice: Assessment, planning, intervention and review*, 3rd edition. Exeter: Learning Matters.

Seligman, M (2002) *Authentic happiness*. London: Nicholas Brealey.

Thompson, N (2006) *People problems*. Basingstoke: Palgrave Macmillan.

Chapter 5

The importance of the perspective of carers and service users

Andy Mantell

Introduction

This chapter will explore reflective practice, with a particular emphasis on the importance of integrating the perspectives of carers and service users, which will be an important part of your social work training. Consequently, the chapter starts by uncovering how the language we use to refer to people is not neutral and can affect our expectations of that relationship.

The experiences of families of people with Huntington's disease are drawn upon to highlight the competing expectations of social work intervention which can be held by families, disabled people and practitioners. The chapter concludes with an exploration of how these expectations can influence the social worker's reflections on the nature and outcomes of their practice.

Huntington's disease is a rare neuro-degenerative condition, which carries a 50 per cent possibility of inheritance from an affected parent. Familial 'carers' can be faced with managing cognitive, motor and behavioural disorders, while uncertain about their own at-risk status. Onset usually occurs from the late thirties to the mid-fifties and life expectancy is approximately 15–20 years.

Telling a story

As you have seen in Chapter 2, reflecting can be viewed as telling a story. In the process of constructing that narrative you are making sense of complex situations and your role within those circumstances. In social work this is not simply a contemplative narrative; social sciences seek to understand social phenomena, but social work also seeks to intervene (Johnsson and Svensson, 2004). Your reflection is therefore purposeful: critical praxis (Rolfe et al., 2010), an ongoing process of improving your actions and decision-making in practice.

Social work intervention has been divided by Parker and Bradley (2010) into four stages: Assessment, Planning, Intervention and Review (ASPIRE). This is not a mechanistic approach, concerned with an expert ticking off each of these stages, but rather it is concerned with 'people not processes' (Skills for Care, 2012); attentive to their interactions, building relationships and the outcomes service users and carers want to achieve. As Maya Angelou (2003, p3, after Buehner 1991, cited in Quote Investigator, 2004) said: *people will forget what you said, people will forget what you did, but people will never forget how you made them feel.* Consequently, these stages have been expanded here to illuminate the accompanying reflective process using Schön's (1983) seminal work. In addition to reflection-in-action, i.e. your thinking at the time, and reflection-on-action, i.e. your thinking afterwards (Johnsson and Svensson, 2004), reflection-before-action is highlighted as essential. In so doing, this chapter seeks to contribute to addressing the challenge of translating theory into practical, effective and empowering solutions for service users (Corey, 2005).

'Reflection' can be viewed as a *generic term for those intellectual and affective activities in which individuals engage to explore their experiences in order to lead to new understandings and appreciations* (Boud and Knight, 1996, p19). Schön (1983) considered this process as *partially beyond conscious articulation*, but it is contended here that reflection and reflexivity (reflection on our reflective process) is a lifelong journey to uncover your motivations for actions in order to consciously influence and justify your practice. As such, reflective practice is an iterative activity which must be experienced rather than abstractly taught.

Naming the characters

The language that we employ to tell a story shapes the images and interpretations that are produced. The main protagonists in this story are called 'carers' and 'service users'. An essential element of reflective practice is to have *a continuous critical dialogue concerning the language we use, deconstructing it and unearthing the assumptions behind its usage* (McLaughlin, 2009, p1114).

ACTIVITY *5.1*

What's in a name?

Write down what the terms 'carers' and 'service users' mean to you.

Write down what these terms imply to you.

Write down your expectations of a carer.

Write down your expectations of a service user.

Now think of a time when you received care from another person. Did you think of that person as a carer and yourself as an actual or potential service user?

Comment

'Carer' is a relational term, in that to be a carer there must be a cared-for person. This oversimplifies the relationship, denies the carer weakness and the cared-for person strength. It ignores the complexity and richness of relationships (Schofield et al., 1998). We actually need to think about care in the wider context of the relationship within which it occurs (Morris, 1993).

RESEARCH SUMMARY

Morris (1993) found that disabled people receiving care from a family member referred to them as 'mother', etc. They talked about their relationships, not about their carers (Morris, 1993, p154). In a qualitative study of carers for people with Huntington's disease, Mantell (2010) found that relatives in the early stages of providing care initially used the same terms, but over time the relationship could change to become dominated by care. In these circumstances spouses valued and felt empowered by viewing themselves as carers.

The term 'carer' was hardly used before the 1970s, but since then the carers' movement has striven for recognition and support for familial carers. The Independent Living Movement, however, questioned the assumption that care should come from the family, arguing that disabled people should be able to manage their own care and employ personal assistants (Morris, 1993). Their campaign has come to partial fruition in the personalisation agenda and the Care Act 2014. Under this Act carers are now eligible for an assessment in their own right. However, carers, perhaps partly due to unfounded but real feelings of guilt or failure, are often reluctant to seek support until they are in crisis. So we need to remain mindful that carers can find themselves trying to assert their needs at a point when they feel least able (Mantell, 2010). Simply put, their voice may not be very loud or they may not tell their story as clearly and calmly as they might wish.

Caring can imply emotional care (Thomas, 1993), i.e. caring about someone (Parker, 1981), and instrumental care (Thomas, 1993), i.e. caring for them (Parker, 1981). The tendency to view these different aspects as synonymous means that a family member's inability to provide physical care may be misconstrued as a negative reflection on their emotional relationship. Family, friends, neighbours and professionals also imbued with this perspective may put additional pressure upon family members to care. If one family member assumes or is given this responsibility, it can assuage the potential obligation of others.

If the term 'carer' speaks of a relationship with a person receiving care, the terms we use for those we provide a service to helps to define that relationship. The term 'client' was widely used in the 1960s, 1970s and 1980s, and is still widely used internationally (McDonald, 2006). However, in the UK, while hinting of early aspirations to therapeutic relationships, it became associated with dependency (McLaughlin, 2009) and viewed as stigmatising. It has since been replaced by a range of terms that are more enlightening about the evolution of social care in the UK than the individuals they are ascribed to.

ACTIVITY **5.2**

Who are you calling a ****?**

The language we use can cause offence. What name would you prefer to be called: 'client', 'consumer', 'customer', 'service user', 'person who uses services' or 'expert by experience'?

Can you think of a better term?

Comment

Each term reflects a different relationship with the individual. The terms 'consumer' and 'customer' indicate progressive shifts towards the marketisation of social care (McLaughlin, 2009, p1104); social workers became care managers and clients became the consumers of their wares, before transforming into customers in a mixed market of state, private and independent services. Social workers have been shifting towards a brokerage role, but they have also remained gatekeepers to resources (Clements, 2011). These terms do not accurately encompass the range of interactions between social workers and the public. It seems a particularly inappropriate reference to apply to the statutory aspects of the social worker's role, for example care proceedings on a young person.

The phrase 'service user' developed from the drive to involve those who use services in their development. 'People who use services' conforms to the People

First Movement's eponymous doctrine of not losing sight of the person, but is unwieldy and risks being reduced to the even more dehumanising acronym PWUS. These phrases can reduce a person's rich social identities to the services they use (McLaughlin, 2009) and consequently perpetuate the view of them as dependent, rather than empowered. As a term it still fails to adequately reflect the subtleties of the social worker's involvement with people, instead, perhaps tellingly, focusing on the resource outcome of involvement.

A recent term that has become widely endorsed is 'experts by experience'; this has the benefit of also including those who were ineligible for services and those who refused services (McLaughlin, 2009). Derived from the disability movement, it encourages a shift from deficit models, in which people who use services are problematised and their views neglected in favour of the expertise of the professional, to strengths-based approaches (Saleebey, 2012), in which they are recognised to have knowledge and expertise too. This name does have its limitations, as the nature and length of experience is variable and experience does not always equate to expertise. Furthermore, the privileging of a person's account due to their experiences is not always desirable, for example the view of a person who abuses children that he does not need intervention (McLaughlin, 2009). However, this term is reflective of social work's concern with 'supporting self-agency and change' (Parton and O'Byrne, 2000, p44) which has evolved 'from a long tradition of anti-oppressive practice' (Sharland and Taylor, 2006, p508). This viewpoint has been gaining wider acceptance in recent social care policy, for example in the personalisation agenda.

Despite this, 'service user' remains the most dominant term in the UK and the one used by the Health and Care Professions Council (2012). Consequently the terms 'service user' and 'carer' are adopted here. However, it must be remembered that the meanings attached to any term are not static; they are dynamic and contested and evolve over time and reveal power in relationships (McLaughlin, 2009). They may initially hold limited or no meaning to those with whom we work, yet can be a crucial label for accessing services. As professionals we must be cautious of our power to label and the access to services labels can confer. We must also remain vigilant to the expectations of role and behaviour that can accompany labels (Becker, 1963).

RESEARCH SUMMARY

Steven Hoskin, a 38-year-old man with learning disabilities, was forced to swallow a lethal dose of paracetamol, was hauled around his bedsit by a dog lead and burned with cigarettes. Then he was frogmarched to the viaduct from where he fell more than 30 metres to his death after Bullock kicked him in the face and stood on his hands *(Valios, 2011). Hoskin had been receiving two hours a week of help from Cornwall Council Adult Services, but cancelled it after Darren Stewart and Sarah Bullock moved into his bedsit. The Serious Case Review (now a Safeguarding Adults Review, under the Care Act 2014) found that* Steven's 'choice' to terminate contact with adult social care was not investigated or explored with him, or other key agencies involved in his care, even though such choices may compound a person's vulnerability; may be made on the basis of inadequate or inappropriate information; or result from the exercise of inappropriate coercion from third parties (Valios, 2011). *It was recommended that where any life-transforming decisions by a known vulnerable adult occurs, this should result in assessments of a person's decision-making capacity.*

Since he was no longer receiving services, Steven was not deemed to be a 'vulnerable adult'. If he had been, then interventions may have prevented his tragic death at the hands of those he thought were his friends. Consequently in the Care Act 2014 safeguarding now applies to those who have need for Care and Support (whether or not the local authority is meeting any of those needs), *are experiencing or at risk of abuse or neglect, and as a result of their care and support needs,* the adult is unable to protect themselves from either the risk of, or the experience of abuse or neglect. *So safeguarding support is now available to a much broader group of people and they no longer need to be labelled as vulnerable, which was problematic as it focused on the individual as being at risk of abuse, rather than wider social and environmental factors (Mantell, 2011).*

Governing variables

Schön (1983) identified that practice is framed by a range of governing variables, which act as limiting factors upon your practice. Legislation, the policies and procedures of employers, instructions from managers, the Health and Care Professions Council standards of conduct, performance and ethics, and the practitioner's own values and ethics all set the parameters within which your interventions occur. In order to empower and engender trust from service users and carers, it is essential to be open and honest about what you can do, but also to challenge limiting factors where necessary.

Pre-assessment

Before you undertake a visit you will need to gather as much information as possible. This is an initial step towards understanding what is going on, a first tentative exploring of the story, reflection-before-action. It is as much hypothetical as fact, questions to be tested when the visit occurs. It is a telling of the anticipated story that is likely to be clouded by governing variables, such as procedures, and your previous experiences of similar situations. This enables you to identify which of your skills and knowledge may be applicable and/or need developing as well as potential weaknesses in past practice you will need to guard against. You are therefore reflecting on the potential limitations of the transferability of skills and knowledge from previous practice to this new situation (Gould, 2004). What skills and knowledge do you need to develop and what mistakes do you need to avoid? This forms part of your ongoing learning process in which you question how emotionally and practically prepared you feel for the unique challenges that you will face.

Huntington's disease is illustrative of numerous rare conditions where workers may lack knowledge. Mantell (2006) found that carers and service users reported professionals adopting several different strategies to address their lack of knowledge. Some proactively sought information, or relied on the carers' knowledge. This could add to the responsibilities upon carers and leave them anxious that there may be key information that they do not know. Other professionals tried to hide their lack of knowledge behind overt displays of being an expert or relying on their usual procedures, leaving carers angry and frustrated (Mantell, 2006). Refusal to acknowledge their lack of knowledge undermined carers' confidence in professionals. In social work we are often in the situation of only holding partial knowledge and must be sensitive to its applicability and potential impact in any given situation. We must also be mindful that even when we reach the point of being experts in a given field, it does not make us an expert on that person's unique circumstances and we must be sensitive to not imposing what we think is best instead of actively listening to them.

Pre-plan and identify strategies

Pre-planning incorporates a further aspect of reflection-before-action, and involves considering various scenarios and corresponding strategies to manage them. When I was a student social worker in a rural team I was asked by a GP to assess a person for attending a day centre. I could not drive and it took me two hours to get there, by which time it was snowing heavily. I knocked and introduced myself and said that I understood that he was interested in day care. He replied 'no' and slammed the door shut. After several more unsuccessful attempts to engage him, I travelled the two hours back. I had gone armed with details of a range of day centres, but it had never occurred to me that I would receive such a blunt response. When I contacted the GP, he informed me that he had not discussed day care with the person, but just thought it might be a good idea.

This example illustrates the importance of checking referral information and the risk of giving too much weight to pre-planning. Pre-plans are at best hypotheses to be tested and agreed with the carer(s) and service user. The expert model is particularly at risk of elevating the importance of the professionals' plans or ignoring the views and feelings of the carer(s) and service users. Heavily bureaucratic organisations can also have a similar impact, skewing the practitioners' focus to the requirements of the agency's systems at the expense of the service user or carers' concerns; as a nurse once told me: 'hitting the target, but missing the point'.

Planning and identifying strategies is primarily an organic process evolving within interactions with agencies, service users and carers. Interventions need to be negotiated rather than pre-ordained if service users and carers are to be empowered. This requires that we advocate for their perspective and where appropriate involve advocates for them, particularly if they lack capacity or have difficulty in participating in the process.

> ### CASE STUDY

Making informed decisions

Cathy (all names have been changed to preserve confidentiality), aged 34, tested negative to carrying the Huntington's disease gene. She had a younger brother who committed suicide (before being aware of the family history of Huntington's disease). Cathy provided care for her mother who lived in a separate home, but following a fall her mother was admitted to hospital and deemed unable to care for herself or live alone any more. In her early fifties, her mother was admitted to a care home for older people. Cathy did not consider that either she or her mother was fully consulted in the process:

> *No, they didn't give me a choice at all. They just said you know we're sticking her in there, because they've got room. No, they didn't ask my opinion, and you know, all I mean, I was relieved I just thought you know thank God for that. And it didn't occur to me to ask any questions like, did they know anything about Huntington's or anything like that.*

> (Mantell, 2006, p146)

> ### ACTIVITY 5.3

(Care) home from home

What good practice steps do you think should be taken to enable a person to enter a care home?

Why do you think that in some situations, such as Cathy's, this good practice does not occur?

What do you think could be done to remedy these difficulties?

Comment

As well as highlighting the importance of engaging with service users and their carers to provide informed choices, Cathy's experiences also demonstrate how the level of choice for specialist provisions can be limited in crisis situations. Proactive planning, such as developing care pathways, is essential to facilitating real choices for people.

Assessment/intervention

Just seeing someone influences their situation. It may, for example, elicit guilt at their behaviour, relief and validation or high expectations that the situation will change (Mantell, 2006). Reflection-in-action forms an integral part of assessment.

A comparison occurs between your expectation of the situation and the actual situation. This adjustment enables a better approximation of the carer's and service user's perspectives to evolve. You are 'reaching for their lived experience and meanings' (Sharland and Taylor, 2006, p508). The assessment may, for example, identify more pressing needs to be met than those previously anticipated. Practitioners have to remain sensitive to the ways in which their preconceived ideas can influence situations. Our assumptions can limit our interpretations of situations and deny individuals the space to express their feelings.

Language and assessment

As we have already seen, assumptions may stem from the language that we assume within professional cultures; for example, within the social care culture individuals within families are identified as carers or service users. Such perceptions can limit our understanding and inhibit our interventions.

Assessments have tended to focus on the quantifiable, instrumental care and can treat carers as care workers with a concern for related issues such as their ability to undertake those tasks, the need for training, for example in manual handling, and being paid to care, for example a carer's allowance. While concern with the burden of care is essential, it can also add to the professionalising (Henderson, 2001) of the carer. As Henderson (2001, p157) stated, being the expert on someone can have a devastating effect on their relationship. Care shifts from being an element of their relationship to defining that relationship, with the service user potentially viewed as a burden (Morris, 1993).

ACTIVITY **5.4**

Who cares?

Do you think that families should be expected to care for their members?

Would you expect a family member or partner to care for you? Would there be a limit to what you would expect or want them to do?

Do you think your expectations would affect your view of members of the family of service users who refuse to provide care?

Comment

Presumptions of care within relationships and attendant judgements that a person does not love their relative if they do not provide care place considerable pressure upon family members, and women in particular, to provide care. Such expectations owe more to the enduring myth of the prevalence of the 'Oxo' family than the diverse reality of relationships. No account is taken of ambivalent or conflictual feelings that can exist within families.

CASE STUDY

Presumptive practice

Martha, aged 22, had a volatile relationship with her mother and had followed her sister's example in leaving home as soon as possible. She was, however, concerned that her mother was neglecting herself, and despite arranging for her to attend a day centre and have a care worker the situation continued to deteriorate. Martha and her elder sister were invited to a meeting at the day centre and were confronted by the spectacle of their mother being asked to perform tests in front of them to demonstrate that she was not well. As Martha pointed out, she was well aware that her mother was not well and did not need to be 'embarrassed' in this way.

Martha was then informed that her mother had Huntington's disease and: 'Oh, by the way, it is hereditary.' While recovering from this shock the sisters were asked which one of them would look after their mother. Neither was in the position to look after their mother, nor did they have the quality of relationship where they would want to provide that care.

It is very easy to become focused upon your own and/or your agency's agenda and achieving your desired outcomes. Such practice becomes oblivious to the context in which interventions occur and the need to be sensitive to the impact of the process of intervention and the contestability of the desired outcomes.

Nolan (2001) argued that mutuality – i.e. reciprocity in the relationship between the carer and service user – is a better determinant of a person's capacity to care than the burden of care. Focusing on mutuality would not only identify if a primary motivator for caring still exists, it also raises the ethical issue of whether people should be expected to provide care if their relationship has changed.

Familial obligation

Care is a gender concept; it is associated with female traits and consequently the expectation of familial care is primarily one of female care. Qureshi and Simons (1987) in their 'hierarchy of obligation' identified how spouses were more likely to provide care than other family members; the next most likely were adult children; same-household members were more likely to care than non-household members; and women are more likely to care than men. Such obligations are strongly defined by the cultural norms of those families, but can be inhibited by prejudice. Families with Huntington's disease, for example, face stigma which can produce secrecy within the family (Mantell, 2006), denying relatives potential support.

Power and assessment

The primary aims of assessment are to find out the stories of those involved in the situation: risk factors, concerns, strengths and what those involved wish to happen. The better the rapport that can be established with those involved, the more forthcoming and comprehensive the story is likely to be. However, the power imbalance between service users, carers and practitioners can inhibit them.

ACTIVITY 5.5

What are the sources of the power imbalance between the practitioner and service user or carer? List as many as you can.

Comment

The power imbalances can be broadly divided into the following:

What you represent to them. This will relate to their previous knowledge of social workers. This may be formed by good or bad previous experiences of social workers and or the public perception of them. I was surprised on a recent visit to Los Angeles to see social work students wearing T-shirts proclaiming their profession. Sadly, this is unlikely to happen in the UK, where press vilification of social workers shows no sign of declining.

As a social worker you also represent authority and this may trigger their feeling towards all figures of authority. This is known as transference and it is possible for us to respond in kind or counter-transference. This may not necessarily be negative responses, but the false expectations then raised can nevertheless be damaging (Lefevre, 2008).

How you look can also trigger transference. You may remind them of their best friend, worst enemy, mother, daughter, etc. The same applies to you, however, so we must be alert to how we are responding to a person to ensure that we are responding to them and not what they represent to you

Why they think/hope you are there. It is worth remembering that they may not share your understanding of why you are there. I once visited a disabled man, who lived in an isolated cottage, and we had our initial conversation through the door (note, not through the letter box, as that is not safe). He thought the social worker's role was to 'take people away'.

If you are there in a statutory capacity, for example for a mental health assessment or child protection investigation, then they may be hostile or resistant, or they demonstrate disguised compliance (Woolmore, 2014), where they seem to be engaging and co-operating but actually are not. Each can limit, disguise or alter the story that is available to you.

They may alternatively think of you in terms of the gatekeeper for a service they desperately require. This can often give workers a power they do not feel.

Where you meet and in what circumstances. Very often when we meet people they are in crisis. This can lead to a narrowing of the focus of their concern. Often it is valuable to let them explore that before broadening the discussion.

Meeting in their house can help them to feel more at ease, but if they are aggressive then meeting in an office is safer. If they are attending a meeting, while this may be intended to be inclusive it can also be intimidating.

It is important to recognise the power difference and be clear about when you may have to do something a person may not want. For example, saying about the limitations of confidentiality at your first visit may make the person more distant from you, but if at a later point you have to share information and they had not been aware this would happen they will be disempowered and feel betrayed.

If a person feels powerless or threatened, then they may try to claim power through being intimidating, aggressive or violent. It is important to respond assertively if someone is intimidating, but if they become aggressive or violent withdraw immediately and contact your manager.

The emerging story is formed from what we know in advance – what we are told by the service user, carer and professionals involved – but also from what we see and smell. We have to be wary of the power imbalance between the accounts of those who are more articulate, assertive and/or have higher social status than others. This is particularly so when working with young children or adults who may have low self-esteem and/or communication difficulties. It also highlights discrepancies and inconsistencies in a situation, which your professional curiosity should prompt you to explore further. This is particularly important where the service user is reluctant to have contact.

ACTIVITY 5.6

Jon Dunicliff, the co-ordinator of Cornwall's Safeguarding Adults Unit, speaking about Steven Hoskin's situation, said: If someone says they don't want a service, you need to look behind that *(Valios, 2011). A similar sentiment was raised in relation to the Serious Case Review into the sexual abuse of 59 young people in Oxford, by groups of men. As well as also recommending a more careful assessment of capacity, the review criticised police and social workers for a lack of professional curiosity (Oxfordshire Safeguarding Children Board, 2015).*

Whether you are students or practitioners, you are busy, and with the pressures upon social care it is likely you will become more busy. How do you remain curious?

Comment

Professional curiosity prompts reflective practice. It is about not taking information at face value, but scrutinising it further. It is also about listening to your gut reaction, that physical feeling that there is something not quite right or some level of incongruity. It requires that we are actively listening and making sense of what we are told. This can be more difficult when we are pressured, but at the point at which we stop doing it we are just going through the motions.

Plan and identify strategies

The core activity of planning and identifying strategies requires reflection-in-action in order to maintain the necessary level of sensitivity to the preferences of all those involved. The exchange model of assessment (Smale et al., 1993) recognises these differences and encourages the exchange of information and negotiation towards consensus on outcomes.

Planning entails thinking about the future, which can be extremely empowering for some carers and service users, enabling them to gain a sense of control. However, for others, particularly families with degenerative diseases, planning means facing the future, which exposes their future loss. Consequently, some carers, such as Tara, who cared for her husband, preferred to focus on the here and now:

> I'd been a great believer, in fact, through Nigel's illness, I take one day at a time. I don't like, I can't think of the future, I don't like to think what the future may hold. I take one day at a time, I get up and just try and get through the day, if it's been a good day, good, and if it's been a bad day, then tomorrow might be better ... And that's how really I've coped with it.

(Mantell, 2006, p215)

ACTIVITY 5.7

Looking to the future

What would be important to talk about with service users and their carers in such circumstances?

How would you feel about having such a conversation? Would there be any topics that you would be nervous or uncomfortable about discussing, such as reduced sexual intimacy or death?

Comment

Your professional and personal perspectives can significantly influence how you explore the future with a service user or carer. What is significant to you may not be as significant to them, or it may hold a much greater significance. The dominance of the medical model can lead professionals to focus on the pathology of a condition, whereas carers focus on the individual affected by the condition recognising their history, their character, their interests and their meaning to the carer. Equally, the social taboo surrounding death in Western society can inhibit the service user, the carer and professional from exploring painful but often necessary issues.

Meetings – 'not about me without me'?

The disability movement coined the phrase 'not about me without me' as a retort to professionals' exclusion of them from processes that were purportedly about them.

Including service users and carers in meetings is the default approach expected in the guidance to the Care Act 2014 (Department of Health, 2014) and is implicit in the principle of working in partnership with families under the Children Act 1989. The eminent Judge Mumby (cited in Lawson et al., 2014) has argued that failing to involve a person in their safeguarding planning under the Care Act could also be a breach of Article 8, the right to private life under the Human Rights Act 1998.

CASE STUDY

Henry is a 28-year-old man who has had a traumatic brain injury as the result of a road traffic incident. He now uses a wheelchair for mobility; he requires two people to help him transfer and has a right-sided weakness in his leg and arm. He has slurred speech and difficulty finding words. He has significant cognitive difficulties, including finding it hard to concentrate and he is easily distracted. His short-term memory is poor and he finds planning difficult. His moods are volatile and he is impulsive. His partner, Molly, would like him to return to their first-floor rented flat. His parents would like him to come home to them. Staff in the independent rehabilitation unit where he has been for the last eight months say he needs to stay there for another three months, and the Clinical Care Group who were funding his placement were reluctant to fund further.

ACTIVITY 5.8

What would you do to involve Henry in his future care planning?

Comment

It is easy to pay lip-service to involving people instead of giving careful consideration how that can best be achieved. It was decided that there needed to be a meeting of all the people involved to try to resolve the issues. However, if Henry had attended the meeting he would have found it overwhelming and distracting, even if he had only attended part of it, and the speech and language therapist considered that he would not understand the key information. Consequently, the speech and language therapist and I met with him before and near the end of the meeting. It was important that this was in his room, away from distractions and where he felt safe, as he was anxious about what would happen. Information was shared in simple short sentences and he was given concrete options to choose from, rather than abstract concepts (such as, 'What would you like to happen?'). He wanted to live with Molly and a plan was developed in the meeting towards that goal. We then checked with him that that was okay, before ending the meeting. This approach could be seen as disempowering, but for Henry it enabled him to take part in the process in a meaningful way. The starting point must be to work towards the outcome the person wants. When working with a child or adult who lacks capacity they should still be involved as much as they can and want, with a focus on their best interest.

Working towards the outcomes a person wants can be particularly difficult where we have a statutory duty. Bull (2013) warned that social workers have a tendency to approach legislation from either a technical perspective, concerned with a detailed understanding of the law; a procedural perspective, matching needs to resources; or with a focus on how rights are supported or eroded by legislation. There are some similarities (if some blurring) between these three approaches and three forms of reflection identified by Taylor (2010). Taylor (2010), drawing on the work of Habermas (1972), identified technical reflection as empirically based, focused on systematic and objective approaches, for example, evidence-based practice. Practical reflections are concerned with our interactions and our expectations of interactions. Consequently our language, as demonstrated above, is a crucial factor in our interpretations of interactions. Finally, emancipatory reflection is concerned with power in interactions and trying to liberate people from constraints, for example, the expert model, situating knowledge and solutions in the hands of the practitioner. A focus on technical and procedural approaches risks the service user or carer perspective becoming peripheral to our actions. However, ignoring these constraining factors could lead to unlawful actions and/or conflict with your employer. As Bull (2013) argued in relation to the legislative approaches, a pragmatic blend of the three forms needs to be developed by each practitioner. Alternatively, seen through the filter of Schön's (1983) learning cycle, each of the three paradigms, within each of the two models, can be seen to be incremental in a journey from single- to double-loop learning. Novice workers tend to focus initially on 'getting it right' – on grasping technical legislation, procedures and ways of interacting effectively. Once these concerns are addressed they may feel better equipped to argue against governing variables, towards a rights/emancipatory approach. However, during their novice period their colleagues should be particularly attentive to their fresh eyes on 'business as usual' and receptive to the challenge they can raise to entrenched practices.

Intervention/assessment

As you shift your focus towards intervention, an ongoing element of assessment is essential. This includes a process of testing those pre-interview hypotheses that still appear applicable and also the generation and testing of new hypotheses. This process of reflection-in-action is concerned with ensuring that the understanding gained is and remains the best possible.

Reflection-in-action (see Chapter 1) is also focused upon the process. How are you interacting and understanding each other? What subtexts are occurring? This requires sensitivity to self as well as to the others present, because communication may be at a non-verbal level. For example, a service user who was depressed spoke to me in a calm quiet manner, but I felt uncomfortable; I was becoming tense. I realised that I was mirroring his tension, which was incongruent to his speech. Transference, i.e. of his tension, and counter-transference, i.e. my becoming tense, are psychoanalytical concepts that can help you to understand your interactions. They also highlight the origin of reflective practice in social work, as derived from its therapeutic tradition.

An important area of reflection is on the extent to which we are empowering the individual to take control and implement change as opposed to us intervening. This is where our original assessment comes to fruition. If we have taken a deficit approach then the individual is likely to be looking to you for solutions and also to hold the responsibility for what happens, whereas a strengths-based approach (Saleebey, 2012) is more likely to have built their confidence and identified ways that they have tackled similar problems before.

Reflection must also become outcome-oriented. Is the intervention still heading in the direction of the agreed objectives? If not, why not? Does it need to be redirected? Or do different objectives need to be identified?

Outcome

The outcome of an intervention triggers reflection-on-action. This again focuses on comparison of the outcome achieved with the outcome sought and consideration of the process. Was it effective? Could it be improved?

A clear distinction needs to be drawn between output and outcome. This is perhaps best explained using the cake analogy (Cook and Miller, 2012). If you imagine making a cake, then the input is the ingredients (or resources) used. Cooking (or activity) is the process, the cake (or service) is the output and the smile on a child's face (or impact on the individual) is the outcome (Cook and Miller, 2012). In reviewing our intervention we must be careful to consider each aspect. It is important not to confuse output and outcome; for example, after being refused a package of care, a carer was told that the assessment *was* the service. The assessment process can be beneficial in itself if the social worker maintains a therapeutic rather than bureaucratic focus.

If we revisit the earlier analogy of a story, Local Authority Social Service Departments have invariably been concerned with tales of needs and risks and how to meet them. The personalisation agenda has seen a change to individuals often undertaking self-assessments and then managing their own personal budget to meet their needs. In the Care Act 2014 there is a shift to outcome-focused assessments being at the heart of self-directed support. Under the Talking Points: Personal Outcomes Approach (POA) developed by the Joint Improvements Team in Scotland, the outcomes of the service user and carer become the primary focus, not those of the organisation. So we start with how the service user and carer want the story to end, rather than how the story started. Cook and Miller (2012) identify personal outcomes for service users and carers as including quality of life, change, and managing the caring role and process – ensuring that they feel listened to and respected.

Review

A review can be seen as a formal process of reflection-on-action including all of the stakeholders. Reviews enable practitioners not only to ascertain whether the outcome has been successful, but also to reflect on how accurately the practitioners' views matched those of the service users, carers and agencies involved.

The review may mark the end of a particular piece of practice or the start of further assessment of unmet needs. Regular reviews are particularly important when working with people with degenerative conditions such as Huntington's disease, where needs may change subtly over time. As Tom found when his wife first started showing symptoms of Huntington's disease:

> *things creep up on you so gradually, things like for instance bottle tops being left undone, a slightly curious walk, the gait changes, the temper gets very slightly sharper, anybody who's experienced PMT would know exactly where we're coming from ... But it starts to multiply you see, and you think, is this right?*

> (Mantell, 2006, p181)

For the practitioner, reviews are also ongoing audit points along with supervision, peer discussion and observation of their reflective process. Such external checks counter the potential neutral (Baldwin, 2004) or insular nature of an individual's reflections, promoting continued learning and development.

Reflection-on-action (see Chapter 1) is about considering how you could have better achieved the objectives of the service users and carers as well as your own. It may be about correcting mistakes or about ways to improve and refine your practice. It is about learning from practice, which can be divided into two forms of learning.

The first is single-loop learning (Argyris and Schön, 1996) and is where you tell the story again considering what you could have done differently to improve the process and outcome. It necessitates that you engaged with the service user and carer to ascertain the outcomes they wanted and that these outcomes were clearly recorded to guide and assess progress (Cook and Miller, 2012).

The second is double-loop learning and is where you go further, to question the governing variables, for example challenging policy, as opposed to implementing them more effectively. As a specialist local authority worker for people with acquired brain injury, I brought to my manager's attention the fact that the eligibility criteria for disabled people did not include cognitive deficits and was therefore an inappropriate assessment tool for a wide range of people. More generally, improvements in developing services can be achieved by collating the information recorded with individuals (Cook and Miller, 2012). However, for double-loop learning (see Chapters 8 and 9) to be achieved, organisations need to encourage such practices (Baldwin, 2004).

As noted earlier, single-loop learning is more associated with student or newly qualified practitioners, as they understandably tend to adhere rigidly to rules. As you engage in post-qualifying training and develop your expertise, you will also tend to incorporate double-loop learning and to integrate single- and double-loop learning into your reflections before and in practice. Expert practitioners also tend towards viewing rules more for guidance than obedience. This discretionary approach reduces insensitive organisational bureaucracy, but necessitates critical reflection to prevent 'street level bureaucracy', i.e. idiosyncratic routines or prejudice aimed at reconciling the conflicting demands of organisations, service users and the practitioner's own value base (Lipsky, 1980).

ACTIVITY **5.9**

Professional discretion

In your practice setting, how much discretion do you have?

How does this compare with your colleagues in other settings?

How does it compare with other professionals with whom you work?

What are the strategies that you adopt to avoid 'street level bureaucracy'?

Comment

The managerial emphasis on quantifiable, evidence-based practice led in the past to a climate of concern with output, throughput and cost which severely restricted professional leeway (Johnsson and Svensson, 2004). Now evidence-based practice, such as the POA, is starting to provide alternatives to social workers, restoring the values and principles of professional practice, which were described as having been diminished through care management and bureaucracy (Miller, 2010, p120).

Understanding and desirable solutions

The model above provides a basic schematic of reflective practice. We tell the story to understand it better and inform our interventions. However, social work is a complex process. We have to be aware that there are multiple perspectives on a situation. Each party in the process has their own understanding of the situation and from that understanding flow their objectives and preferred solutions. For example, Karen cared for her husband Ralph but they had different views about how that care should be provided:

> *I might have been able to manage at home if he would be willing to have a nurse, or carers come in to help me. But he will not let them in the house.*

(Mantell, 2006, p164)

ACTIVITY **5.10**

Who's right?

Whose rights should prevail in circumstances like those of Karen and Ralph?

Comment

In my experience, the views of the service user tend to prevail in the short term, but if their carer reaches a point of being unable to continue, the service user may find that they are admitted to a care home, in a crisis situation, with limited choices. Central to this undesired outcome is the service user's level of mental capacity. Huntington's disease, for example, can cause rigidity of thinking, limiting the person's ability to consider alternatives. Advance planning may enable consensus to be achieved, but in some with conditions such as dementia or acquired brain injury, the person may lack insight into their needs. The provisions of the Mental Capacity Act 2005 has the potential to promote the views of service users through advanced decisions to refuse treatment, but also to shift authority to the views of the carer when the service user's level of capacity is in doubt, through lasting powers of attorney, for example.

Social workers therefore need to develop a multi-sited understanding of a situation in order to recognise that meaning is constructed by multiple agents in varying contexts or places (Marcus, 1998, p52). Social workers' ability to draw on a range of social sciences potentially increases their sensitivity to different approaches compared with those from more defined traditions.

In working with families there is often an implicit assumption that consensus is achievable, but this may not be possible. In such circumstances, whose meanings and, consequently, objectives are we aiming to meet? A relative of a service user who was a solicitor once said to me: 'Who is your client?' I replied that they both were. She was identifying a potential conflict of interest. One of the criticisms of social work has been the focus on one family member's needs to the detriment of another, for example in Victoria Climbié's case.

Reflection is fundamentally about making the implicit explicit in order to critically scrutinise practice. Practitioners need to recognise and value different people's objectives but be explicit about whose objectives are being prioritised and, where appropriate, identify support or advocates for the other family members. This is not a straightforward process, as whose needs are paramount may change over time. One solution would be for social workers to move away from the terminology of carer and service user to identifying a 'primary client', who remains the focus of their intervention. As the shift to individualised budgets proceeds, service users may demand that level of focus on their needs.

Time after time

Your first assessments may tend towards the mechanistic as you strive to become familiar with and master its components. Eventually, undertaking and reflecting on an assessment will become fluid, so much so that there is a risk of taking it for granted. Where this happens it is easy to find yourself going through the motions, hearing what you expect to hear and responding to situations you have seen, rather than are seeing. This is more likely where you are faced repeatedly with similar situations. As Taylor (2000, p239) remarked: *It is easy to do something when it is novel. It is another thing to maintain something when it has lost some of its initial appeal.* The reflective answer is to set an internal alarm bell to ring when situations seem the same, because while situations may be similar, the individuals going through them are unique. At such points it is essential to ensure you are actively rather than passively listening and that you remain receptive and curious about what you are hearing. My doctoral thesis was entitled 'Huntington's disease: The carers' story', because their stories were not being heard.

Taoists have a notion of 'the beginner mind', encountering all situations as if for the first time. Taking such a curious, beginner's mind will not only help you to stay receptive to service users and their carers, but will also help you to appreciate the world around you and reduce your own stress.

CHAPTER SUMMARY

This chapter has highlighted the reflective process that coexists with social work practice. It has drawn on the example of people with Huntington's disease and their families to illustrate that the objectives of intervention are not always straightforward. Multi-sited meaning creates multi-sited objectives. Reflective practice enables social workers to develop the capacity for the creative (Trevithick, 2005) and for discretionary practice to meet people's diverse demands. However, you need to be sensitive to your use of language and reflective on your own agenda(s). It is essential to be explicit about whose objectives you are prioritising and the assumptions you may be making:

With care in the community of course, there's much more it being expected and assumed you're carers. And it's not always right.

(Susan, who cared for her husband, in Mantell, 2006, p177)

FURTHER READING

Cottrell, S (2005) *Critical thinking skills*. Basingstoke: Palgrave.

Excellent introductory text for developing your analytical skills.

Gould, N and Baldwin, M (eds) (2004) *Social work, critical reflection and the learning organisation*. Aldershot: Ashgate.

Slightly more advanced text on reflective practice in social work.

Gould, N and Taylor, I (eds) (1996) *Reflective learning for social work*. Aldershot: Ashgate.

Excellent introductory text to reflective practice in social work.

Miller, E (2012) *Individual outcomes: Getting back to what matters*. Edinburgh: Dunedin Academic Publications.

An accessible introduction to the POA.

Parker, J and Bradley, G (2010) *Social work practice: Assessment, planning, intervention and review*, 3rd edition. Exeter: Learning Matters.

Read the original model, expanded upon within this chapter.

REFERENCES

Argyris, C and Schön, D (1996) *Organisational learning II*. Boston: Addison Wesley.

Baldwin, M (2004) Critical reflection: opportunities and threats to professional learning and service development in social work organisations. In N Gould and M Baldwin (eds), *Social work, critical reflection and the learning organisation*. Aldershot: Ashgate.

Becker, H (1963) *Outsiders: Studies in the sociology of deviance*. New York: Free Press.

Boud, D and Knight, S (1996) Course design and reflective practice. In N Gould and I Taylor (eds), *Reflective learning for social work*. Aldershot: Ashgate.

Bull, S (2013) Applying legislation in social work. In A Mantell (ed.), *Skills for Social Work*. London: Sage.

Clements, L (2011) *Social care law developments: A sideways look at personalisation and tightening eligibility criteria*. Available at: www.lukeclements.co.uk/resources-index/files/PDF%2002.pdf (accessed 24.5.2013).

Cook, A and Miller, E (2012) *Talking points: Personal outcome approach*. Available at: www.jitscotland.org.uk/action-areas/talking-points-user-and-carer-involvement/ (accessed 24.5.2013).

Corey, G (2005) *Theory and practice of counselling and psychotherapy*, 7th edition. Belmont, CA: Brooks/Cole.

Department of Health (2014) *Care and support statutory guidance: issued under the Care Act 2014*. Available from www.gov.uk/government/publications/care-act-2014-statutory-guidance-for-implementation

Gould, N (2004) Introduction: The learning organisation and reflective practice – The emergence of a concept. In N Gould and M Baldwin (eds), *Social work: Critical reflection and the learning organisation*. Aldershot: Ashgate.

Habermas, J (1972) *Knowledge and human interests* (trans J Shapiro). London: Heinemann.

Health and Care Professions Council (2012) *Standards of conduct, performance and ethics*. London: HCPC.

Henderson, J (2001) He's not my carer – he's my husband: personal and policy constructions of care in mental health. *Journal of Social Work Practice*, 15(2): 149–59.

Johnsson, E and Svensson, K (2004) Theory in social work: some reflections on understanding and explaining interventions. *European Journal of Social Work*, 8(4): 419–33.

Lawson, J, Lewis, S and Williams C (2014) *Making safeguarding personal guide 2014*. Available from: www.local.gov.uk/...Safeguarding (accessed 28/8/15)

Lefevre, M (2008) *Communicating with children and young people*. Bristol: Policy Press.

Lipsky, M (1980) *Street-level bureaucracy: Dilemmas of the individual in public service*. New York: Russell Sage Foundation.

Mantell, A (2006) *Huntington's disease: The carers' story*. Unpublished DPhil thesis, University of Sussex.

Mantell, A (2010) Under a cloud: carers' experiences of Huntington's disease. *Social Care and Neurodisability*, 1(2): 33–41.

Mantell, A (2011) Introduction. In T Scragg and A Mantell (eds) *Safeguarding adults in social work*, 2nd edition. Exeter: Learning Matters.

Marcus, G (1998) *Ethnography through thick and thin*. New Jersey: Princeton Publications.

McDonald, C (2006) *Challenging social work: The context of practice*. Basingstoke: Palgrave Macmillan.

McLaughlin, H (2009) What's in a name: 'client', 'patient', 'customer', 'consumer', 'expert by experience', 'service user' – what's next? *British Journal of Social Work* 39(6): 1101–17.

Miller, E (2010) Can the shift from needs-led to outcomes-focused assessment in health and social care deliver on policy priorities? *Research, Policy and Planning*, 28(2): 115–27.

Morris, J (1993) *Independent lives: Community care and disabled people*. London: Macmillan.

Nolan, M (2001) The positive aspects of caring. In S Payne and C Ellis-Hill (eds), *Chronic and terminal illness: New perspectives on caring and carers*. Oxford: Oxford University Press.

Oxfordshire Safeguarding Children Board (2015) *Serious case review into child sexual exploitation in Oxfordshire: from the experiences of children A, B, C, D, E, and F*. Available from: www.oscb.org.uk/.../ SCR-into-CSE-in-Oxfordshire (accessed 28/8/15).

Parker, J and Bradley, G (2010) *Social work practice: Assessment, planning, intervention and review*, 3rd edition. Exeter: Learning Matters.

Parker, R (1981) Tending and social policy. In E Goldman and S Hatch (eds), *A new look at the personal social services*. London: Policy Studies Institute.

Parton, N and O'Byrne, P (2000) *Constructive social work: Towards a new practice*. London: Macmillan.

Quote investigator (2014) Available from: http://quoteinvestigator.com/2014/04/06/they-feel/#note-8611-15

Qureshi, H and Simons, K (1987) Resources within families: caring for elderly people. In J Brannen and G Wilson (eds), *Give and take in families: Studies in resource distribution*. London: Allen and Unwin.

Rolfe, G, Jasper, M and Freshwater, D (2010) *Critical reflection in practice: Generating knowledge for care*. London: Palgrave Macmillan.

Saleebey, D (2012) *The strengths perspective in social work practice*. Boston, MA: Pearson.

Schofield, H, Bloch, S, Herman, H, Murphy, B, and Nankervis, J (eds) (1998) *Family caregivers: Disability, illness and ageing*. Melbourne: Allen and Unwin.

Schön, D (1983) *How professionals think in action*. New York: Basic Books.

Sharland, E and Taylor, I (2006) Social care research: a suitable case for systematic review. *Evidence & Policy*, 2(4): 503–23.

Skills for Care (2012) *Workforce Development 55: People not processes: The future of personalisation and independent living*. Available from: www.scie.org.uk/publications/reports/ report55/ (accessed 28/8/15).

Smale, G, Tuson, G, Biehal, N and Marsh, P (1993) *Empowerment, assessment, care management and the skilled worker*. National Institute for Social Work Practice and Development Exchange. London: HMSO.

Stone, E (2012) *Social care white paper*. Available at: www.jrf.org.uk/blog/2012/07/social-care-white-paper (accessed 24.5.2013).

Taylor, B (2000) *Reflective practice: A guide for nurses and midwives*. Buckingham: Open University Press.

Taylor, B (2010) *Reflective practice for health care professionals*, 3rd edition. Maidenhead: Open University Press

Thomas, C (1993) De-constructing concepts of care. *Sociology*, 27(4): 649–69.

Trevithick, P (2005) *Social work skills: A practice handbook*, 2nd edition. Maidenhead: Open University Press.

Valios, N (2011) Five years on from Steven Hoskin has safeguarding improved? *Community Care*, 29/6/11. Available from: www.communitycare.co.uk/2011/06/29/five-years-on-from-steven-hoskin-has-safeguarding-improved/ (accessed 2/8/15).

Woolmore, S (2014) Sue Woolmore talks about disguised compliance and professional curiosity. From the Safeguarding Children E-academy, available from: www.safeguardingchildrenea.co.uk/resources/sue-woolmore-talks-about-disguised-compliance-2/ (accessed 17/12/15).

Chapter 6

Reflection and avoiding professional dangerousness

Sandra Wallis

Introduction

This chapter relates the concept of reflective practice to that of professional dangerousness. In today's modern society citizens place their trust in those professionals charged with providing welfare. When things go wrong with this provision, there is often a public inquiry into the circumstances surrounding the incident. This is the fourth edition of *Reflective Practice in Social Work* and there have been many examples of bad practice in the intervening years. For children's services we had inquiries into the tragic deaths of Victoria Climbié (Laming, 2003) and Baby 'P' (www.dcsf.gov.uk/swtf) and in adult care numerous reports on failed residential services. The National Health Service came under fire with the highly critical inquiry report into the standard of care at Mid-Staffordshire Hospital Trust (www.midstaffspublicinquiry.com). The Inquiry reported several years after the initial concerns were raised and exemplified how these processes have tended to become long, drawn out, expensive and intensely bureaucratic. The report listed 290 separate recommendations which have been accepted by the government. Putting these into practice will undoubtedly put more pressure onto an already over-burdened workforce. We wait to see how these recommendations are translated into practice, especially as the NHS is currently undergoing extensive changes amid funding cuts.

This is one of the latest of a long line of inquiry reports that have highlighted dangerous instances within the social care sector where the professionals involved have lost a sense of perspective in complex and challenging situations. The police have recently come under fire for their handling of large-scale child sexual exploitation cases in Rotherham and elsewhere in the country. On the positive side, the publication and implementation of the Care Act 2014 promises to bring all the disparate legislation surrounding adult social care together under one umbrella.

Within children's social care, the government set up a task force to look at the effect of over-bureaucratisation on social work practice (Department of Education, 2010). This task force had been set up in the wake of the Climbié case (Laming, 2003) and this led to Professor Munro being asked to review child protection procedures in England and Wales. Her report noted the way that the system has become over-proceduralised, with a target mentality and a focus on performance indicators. She cautioned that when an organisation does not pay sufficient attention to communication skills, procedure may be followed in a way that is technically correct but so incompetent that the desired results are not achieved. She also reported that previous inquiries into high-profile child abuse cases tended to focus on aspects of professional error without addressing the causes (Munro, 2011).

Indeed, the dominant response to those reports dealing with the deaths of children in child protection cases has been a rational bureaucratic one of developing the law, procedures and performance management in an attempt to avoid future catastrophes. In the process, attention to the psychological and emotional aspects of doing social work has been squeezed out. A feature of many of the reports is the numerous recorded instances where the failure of individual workers to carry out what seem to be quite simple tasks has contributed to the death of the child. There have been very few attempts at explaining these failures to act in terms of the feelings of the workers involved. To some extent, we in social work education have compounded this neglect with our emphasis on rights and empowerment and anti-oppressive practice without attending to what are the very real challenges of working with often aggressive and hostile involuntary clients – who do not want a service and make up a significant amount of statutory work. This view is one endorsed by Donald Forrester and his colleagues, writing about the difficulties experienced by social workers working with parents in child protection cases (Forrester et al., 2008).

The Department of Education published *Policy Paper: 2010 to 2015 government policy: children's social workers* (updated 8 May 2015) (www.gov.uk/government/publications/2010-to-2015-government-policy-childrens-social-workers/2010-to-2015-government-policy-childrens-social-workers). This partial response to Munro's report starts off by stating that nearly 600,000 children were referred to local authority children's services because of concerns about their welfare. It goes on to say that it is the role of social workers to lead the assessment of the needs of these children and make sure effective action is taken quickly to protect them from harm. Included in the policy guidance was the provision of a 'Panel of Independent Experts' to provide advice to local safeguarding boards – more supervision of professionals, seemingly without a thought of the resource implications of local authorities' children's services working with 600,000 referrals a year. This statement goes alongside government funding cuts of 40 per cent imposed on local authorities. The policy paper was to be implemented alongside the new *Working Together to Safeguard Children* document 2015 (www.gov.uk/government/publications/working-together-to-safeguard-children--2).

The central purpose of this chapter is to improve our practice by reflecting on the feelings involved in our dealings with these and other families. In particular, the focus is on how to avoid acting in ways that can, albeit unintentionally, actually work so as to increase the risk of dangerousness. Such self-defeating practices have been grouped together under the term 'professional dangerousness'. Although these practices can occur within any area of social work, this part of the book will deal with the effect they have on child protection work. An early comment from a fellow social work educator on the ideas behind this chapter said: *But I do not think that the concept of professional dangerousness will mean much to social work students and may actually be rather alarming and therefore off-putting to them.* My own view is that on the contrary it is important for social workers and students to be able to face up to and discuss, analyse and reflect upon the issue of dangerousness in our profession in order that it can be understood and so allow us to avoid some of the worst pitfalls associated with it.

The important part played by reflective practice in improving the social work task is the central theme of this book and has already been dealt with extensively. This chapter is one of those charged with developing this theme into various practice areas. In it I suggest some ways whereby practitioners might reflect upon the idea of 'professional dangerousness' as a way of improving practice. The first part is quite brief and covers and sometimes extends only those parts of reflective practice that appear relevant to this undertaking. The main part of the chapter explains and explores the concept of professional dangerousness and relates this to the practice of reflection within the social work task.

Reflective practice

In the introductory chapter we looked at how we might improve our professional practice in terms of Schön's *reflection-on-action* and *reflection-in-action*. The first involves us in thinking back on something already done, away from the action itself. The second, reflection-in-action, refers to thinking about what you are doing while you are doing it. As Schön himself says, *phrases like thinking on your feet, keeping your wits about you, and learning by doing suggest not only that we can think about doing but that we can think about doing something while doing it* (1991, p54).

Thompson (2009) has recommended that we add a third concept here and reflect on our practice before, during and after the event. How then do these three concepts – reflection-before-action, reflection-in-action and reflection-on-action – relate to social work practice? Reflective practice is a dynamic concept and I think that the doing of 'good' social work has to mean that the social worker is continuously engaged in a process of reflective activity that includes all three of these elements. For us, reflection-before-action involves us in gathering together and appraising what information is available both at the start of a case and throughout all of our involvement with the service user. Reflection-in-action means always keeping the situation under constant review and revising or modifying our strategy as a result of these reflections. Reflection-on-action allows us to learn from the experience so that we can benefit from any insights and use these to inform our future practice.

This need for continuous reflecting on practice can perhaps best be shown if we look very briefly at some of the dynamics operating within the Victoria Climbié case (Laming, 2003). Here, for example, a file had initially been opened on the case as an asylum-seeking homeless family, so those involved would be viewing it in the context of the department's rules and policies for this group of people – concerning issues of homelessness and immigration. At this early stage, reflection-before-action on the part of the social worker allocated the case and others involved would have been around these policies. As the case progressed (reflection-in-action) and additional information started arriving – for example, one worker's description of the child as looking like an Oxfam poster – this may have helped to trigger the workers into seeing this as a child protection case which required a conference, had they reflected on the situation. By continuously reflecting-on-action the social worker may also have been able to recognise how her own and others' reactions to dealing with the case – feelings of distaste and intimidation when confronting the carers, the problem of language, the failure to acknowledge the 'stage-managed' visits – were all deflecting from the real need to protect Victoria from danger. Had this case been one where the social worker involved and those supervising her had been able to reflect on their practice in these ways it may have led to an important change of direction.

Crucially, the process of reflection must also include an appraisal of whatever relevant research evidence is available, as well as ongoing references to the experiences of colleagues/supervisors as a guide to practice. I conducted a two-year project aimed at improving social work practice which involved giving child care social work teams the opportunity to discuss and reflect on their current cases through applying relevant and up-to-date research to their practice. This was mainly done by way of finding, accessing, reading and critically appraising likely relevant journal articles and applying them to their cases. An unintended but beneficial consequence of the project was that the process allowed the social workers time to reflect on their 'live' cases (Wallis, 2004). In short, as was concluded in Chapter 1, it emphasised that social workers need to be *informed reflective practitioners*.

CASE STUDY

An example of reflection-on-action is given in the following extract. It is taken from a post-qualified social worker's notes reflecting on a recent child protection case.

Although I met with JoJo regularly to try to ascertain her views, looking back I think that if I had undertaken more structured sessions with her, for example individual work, I would possibly have gained more insight. I have to challenge myself and ask why I chose not to do this; is it because of restrictions of time, is it because I lack experience and confidence in this area, or is it because of knowing that JoJo's mother may not be happy with this way of assessing. I think it is probably a combination of all three.

The time element is a real factor working with busy caseloads, however (if) it produces better outcomes in the long run, then I feel it is beneficial and worth putting in the time.

I lack experience, which affects my confidence. However, I recognise that the only way I am going to develop in this area and gain confidence is to practise.

As for the third reason, I have to remember that although I am trying to build up a working relationship with Mum, I am first and foremost JoJo's Social Worker and she is the priority.

ACTIVITY 6.1

After you have read the above reflections, make a note of your answers to the following questions:

- *The social worker has developed the habit of being quite critical of her own behaviour, in this case where she was asked to contribute an assessment. Why do you think this may be an important skill?*

- *Why does the social worker feel that she should have 'undertaken more structured sessions' with JoJo?*

- *What are the three reasons given for not doing this?*

Comment

Now think about your answers. This social worker has developed the habit of reflecting on her practice so as to look for clues about what is happening in the child's family. In terms of assessing the relationships within the family, why is the failure of the social worker to work with JoJo on her own likely to be dangerous for JoJo? You might also consider why it could have been dangerous for the social worker to have worked with JoJo on her own.

Do you think that this practitioner will now improve her practice as a result of this reflective activity?

So what is 'professional dangerousness'?

Professional dangerousness can occur when workers responsible for child protection leave a child at risk of significant harm as a consequence of their assumptions, attitudes or behaviour.

It can be defined as:

> the process by which individual workers or multi-disciplinary networks can, mostly unwittingly, act in such a way as to collude with, maintain or increase the dangerous dynamics of the family. (Reder and Duncan, 1999)

The above definition points to twin aspects of professional dangerousness. The first is the process by which 'individual workers' can act in so-called dangerous ways. This aspect I will call 'dangerous behaviour'. The second aspect, where the contribution to dangerousness is by 'multi-disciplinary networks', I will call 'organisational dangerousness'.

Dangerous behaviour

In child care, professional dangerousness can occur when workers responsible for child protection leave a child at risk of significant harm as a consequence of their assumptions, attitudes or behaviour. Those involved frequently experience feelings of acute danger when facing hostile families, and can react irrationally to it. Aggressive or hostile behaviour towards social workers is like the elephant in the room; although everyone knows it is there, it is rarely addressed. There are very real problems arising from practitioners not feeling able to reflect upon and discuss their fears, and uncomfortable feelings about such experiences.

Some commentators have described these feelings. One remarks on the:

> infantile anxieties, which the task of child protection evokes in staff. Feelings of helplessness, of dependence and deference to authorities, of not knowing enough, of sticking to rules like a terrorised child, of fear and wanting to return to the normal world as soon as possible.

(Rustin, 2005)

Another has described his feelings when reacting to the danger in his early days as a social worker:

> *That sense in which you are so preoccupied with your own safety and survival that the safety and survival of the child becomes an afterthought, where just getting out of the house alive or relatively unscathed becomes the defining criteria of a good intervention – but of course this is never made explicit. Or when not seeing the child becomes not a source of concern, but a relief – in fact you have written to the family to pre-announce your visit not as a strategy to ensure they are there, but (un)consciously to sabotage the visit by giving them a chance to be out, or hiding in the house when you call. And when you knock and there's no reply, you skip back up the path and suddenly the world seems like a better place again, all because you don't have to struggle through another tortuous session with angry parents or carers.* (Ferguson, 2005)

Most families signal their distress that they are on the brink of a dangerous crisis in advance, if only what is being communicated can be understood. It takes professional skill to recognise the clues that are being given out in such cases and this skill needs careful development if it is to flourish and be sustained. We can miss even fairly basic clues if we don't reflect carefully on our practice. One 'paper' example of how, without careful reflection, simple clues can be missed in what was a relatively straightforward case comes from a social worker's case study report. Here the writer evinced 'surprise' when a parent withdrew from a care plan of rehabilitation. This reaction came about even though the social worker's own earlier case notes clearly showed the parent's increasing lack of motivation and focus with the plan – important clues signalling the upcoming withdrawal. Social workers visiting a family in a potentially fraught child abuse case where the carers are hostile and aggressive can react in many of the irrational ways described above. In so reacting they miss the clues and are unable (or unwilling) to decode the meaning of what is being communicated and thus cannot remain focused on the child's situation.

Social workers and students on placement have a responsibility to keep safe that entails a knowledge of self and an awareness and sensitivity to recognise situations where you or others may be intimidated or hurt. If you miss the clues you may well inflame an already hostile situation and escalate the aggression, resulting in you or a service user being harmed.

What counts as threatening behaviour?

We have all encountered threatening behaviour at some time or other – some more than others. According to one commentator, hostile and aggressive acts include the following: shouting, swearing, using abusive language, taking up an aggressive stance, e.g. jabbing a finger in the face, making verbal threats in person or in writing, spitting, invasion of personal space, unwanted touching, throwing objects, brandishing a weapon, hitting, other physical or sexual attacks, preventing someone from leaving, damaging property (Koprowska, 2005).

ACTIVITY **6.2**

Look at Koprowska's above list of hostile and aggressive acts.

- *Make a note of those acts that you have experienced that were directed at you.*
- *Go through these acts indicating which acts you experienced most often – trying to remember how you reacted.*
- *Indicate which one of these acts (e.g. shouting?) you found the most frightening and how you reacted in those situations.*

Now think again about the acts on Koprowska's list.

- *Make a second list of those acts that you have witnessed that were directed at some-one else.*
- *Which one of these have you witnessed most often and what was your reaction?*
- *Which of these frightened you the most?*

Comment

Looking back on these experiences, do you think there were times when there were some clues about impending violent behaviour that you missed? Often, when we are really frightened by such irrational behaviour we tend to react irrationally to it. Did your most frightening experience occur when there was just you and the aggressor, or was there a group? It seems that some of the most violent acts of aggression occur within groups when the perpetrator is 'egged on'. Was the act that occurred the most the same as the one that frightened you most? If we experience bad behaviour often enough we tend to accept it as normal. Looking at your second list, was the act that frightened you most the same as the one in your first list? How did you react to this situation? We quite naturally tend to feel less threatened and perhaps even slightly relieved when the hostile act is directed at someone else rather than at us.

If you compare your answers to Activity 6.2 to a colleague's answers you may well find that their answers are different from yours. We each react differently because of the prior experiences that we bring to each encounter and also according to our particular feelings at the time. Those of us who experienced excessive bullying at school, for example, may well view physical attacks as the most frightening aspect of aggressive behaviour and it is indeed these kinds of threats that generally evoke patterns of irrational behaviour on our part.

ACTIVITY **6.3**

Can you recall a recent situation when you felt intimidated by the likely aggressive or violent behaviour of someone or something? Think of those times at home or at school or at work when you felt physically threatened by someone else's behaviour. Perhaps

---

this happened when you were travelling on public transport or when confronted with somebody who was drunk? A good example of this would be if as a car user you had experience of 'road rage'.

Write down your answers to the following questions:

1. *What was it about the behaviour that made you feel intimidated?*

2. *Did it tend to make you react aggressively?*

3. *Did this sort of situation happen quite often or was it unusual?*

4. *Was this a situation that surprised you or did you expect it to happen?*

5. *Were there any clues to warn you that this might happen?*

6. *What did you do about it?*

7. *Did anyone else intervene?*

8. *Did your/their reaction make the situation worse or better?*

9. *How did you avoid it happening again?*

10. *What lessons did you learn from the experience?*

Comment

Think about your answers. Maybe there were some clues leading up to the altercation that you missed because you were too apprehensive? This can happen quite often in stressful situations. Did you feel unable to do anything or did you have a protective strategy to deal with it? Reacting aggressively when feeling intimidated is not unusual although it generally escalates the violence. If it is something that occurred often (repetitive) or something you expected to happen (predictable) then you might have come to accept the behaviour as quite normal and not been particularly worried by it. The situation would have got even more inflamed or else perhaps defused depending on your and other people's reactions. One way of avoiding it happening again is to make sure you avoid that person in the future or else put into practice some of the lessons you learned from the encounter.

Compare your answers with a colleague or fellow student. Do you both have similar answers or do you find you each have different coping strategies?

These understandings can all be applied to the concept of professional dangerousness as this relates to our practice. Reflection-on-action in this way about what happened/happens in our encounters with service users helps us to be more aware that our protective intentions and actions can inadvertently contribute to extending dangerous behaviour in some families. As Howe has theorised:

> *The defence mechanisms used by all of us at some time or other have their origins in (these) early attempts to cope with anxiety, abandonment, loss, conflict and*

emotional pain. In essence, the defences we use involve either (i) keeping painful information out of consciousness (for example denial and avoidance mechanisms) or (ii) redefining or trying to control painful experiences (for example projecting one's anger on to others and blaming them). One way of coping with these conflicting feelings is simply to try and avoid the conflict. Parents who cannot visit their sick children in hospital or social workers who make excuses not to see difficult clients are practicing avoidance.

(Howe, 1995, p93)

We know too that our professional practices (and systems) can mirror the very family patterns that we hope to change, so that we start to behave in the same way as the families we deal with by perhaps accepting their abusive behaviour as 'normal'. This mirroring can also be mimicked within the workplace by creating 'scapegoats' to excuse unacceptable practices. A colleague in another agency may be blamed for what he or she did or did not do, or a more junior colleague may be blamed for their lack of skill or expertise.

While not wishing to be alarming, there is no getting away from the fact that social workers often encounter hostility and aggression in their dealings with service users. Aggression may be directed towards family members, other service users, social workers or other professionals. In the course of his reflections on the Victoria Climbié case, Ferguson (2005) notes that while stress and violence in social work have been the subjects of important commentary, the sheer scale of resistance and hostility that professionals have to bear, particularly in child protection and its implications, requires further recognition.

Ferguson and O'Reilly (2001) reported that their study of all child care referrals made to three social work teams over a three-month period revealed high levels of resistance, intimidation and violence against social workers. In at least 34 per cent of all cases that the social workers worked with they defined the parents or carers as involuntary clients who did not want a service. A powerful theme to emerge was the level of workers' anxiety not only for children's safety but for their own safety and wellbeing.

It is vital to remember, though, that generally encounters between social workers and service users are not characterised by hostility. Many service users in all fields engage with services on a voluntary basis and get on well with their workers. Nonetheless, high numbers of staff across the whole social care workforce have experienced some form of aggression from service users, to the extent that *social care staff have the lead position in being the most abused profession as compared to any other comparable working group* (Braithwaite, 2001, p5).

Ways of dealing with such hostility and aggression centre on reflection-before-action, whereby safety can be improved both for the social worker and the child by good planning and anticipation, as well as reflection-on-action where the learning of good interpersonal skills for recognising and dealing with aggression are paramount. In such situations, the confrontational aspect between social worker and carer can often severely limit the available strategies for changing behaviour through reflection-in-action (thinking on your feet). Schön has acknowledged this likely limitation and notes that what he calls *the action present (the period of time in which we remain in the same situation) varies greatly from case to case and in many cases there is time to think what we are doing* (1991, p278). He concludes: *Indeed, our conception of the art of practice ought to give a central place to the ways in which practitioners learn to create opportunities for reflection-in-action* (1991, p279). As social work practitioners we need to always be on the lookout for strategies that allow us to reflect and review our practice in the light of new information.

Organisational dangerousness

From our original definition, organisational dangerousness covers the processes by which organisations, albeit unwittingly, act in such a way as to collude with, maintain or increase the dangerous dynamics of the family. Often, this form of professional dangerousness goes unrecognised because it is embedded in the culture of the organisation. Ruch (2002) considers that the importance of the concept of reflective practice to social work is that it permits a holistic understanding of the knowledge generation process and stresses the importance of attending to both rational and irrational responses to practice encounters. Interestingly, in giving an example of the difference between the two responses, she describes a situation of organisational dangerousness in child care practice involving a family with a history of sexually abusive relationships, where the departmental 'rational' response to concerns was to repeatedly devise ever more complex written agreements, as if these would safeguard the child concerned in what was becoming an increasingly 'irrational' situation.

A further example is where a charitable organisation is blinded to racism by its own culture, as described in a book by Gould and his colleagues. Here, a voluntary agency working in the homeless sector was unable to recognise that it was the agency's white, middle-class, female culture that made it unable to appreciate the problems with clients that their black reception staff faced (Gould and Baldwin, 2004, p146).

Yet other instances of organisational dangerousness occur when a bureaucratic procedural response to a perceived problem can actually make a situation worse. There are other ways by which an institutional culture can work against good practice, particularly when, as now, social work departmental guidelines are dictated by resources, and this can mean that social workers lose focus and apply the perceived needs of the service user to the eligibility criteria instead of what may be required in the care plan. This typically draws a response of 'well, we know there's no money in the kitty', and points to a culture of inevitability and belief that 'this is just part of the job' that is present in many social service agencies.

CASE STUDY

Eight-year-old Victoria Climbié died in February 2000 from hypothermia, malnutrition and physical abuse suffered at the hands of her carers: a great-aunt and her cohabitee. The great-aunt brought Victoria from the Ivory Coast to France and then to London, supposedly to improve her education. During the last ten months of her life, Victoria

(Continued)

CASE STUDY *continued*

had been known to the social services departments of four local authorities and two police child protection teams and admitted with suspected non-accidental injuries to the paediatric wards of two different hospitals in the space of ten days.

The Climbié Report (Laming, 2003) notes that on many occasions, although various professionals from all disciplines had information concerning Victoria's plight, they did not act on it. Many reasons have been put forward to explain why what was seen to be an overworked and under-supported workforce failed to act. But it has also been suggested that this kind of paralysis was due to the underlying psychological and emotional dynamics of the impact of having to work with violent clients (Ferguson, 2005). In relation to social work practice, we can see this failure to act in the way that many of the proposed visits to the family by social services and the police did not take place. The report describes Kouao and Manning (the carers) as being routinely aggressive and menacing and also how they were able to stage-manage the pre-announced visits to the flat. The combined effect was that although by this time agencies were concerned enough to consider a visit, Victoria was never interviewed. There were in addition communication/language problems that were never resolved – the family spoke French.

The professional dangerousness exhibited here was at two levels. First, as in this case, all of those involved in such situations feel intimidated by the aggressive behaviour of the carers and seek to avoid contact with the family because of this. Second, this avoidance strategy is compounded by an element of distaste and fear brought about by the condition of the family. Victoria was diagnosed early on in the case as having scabies – and two social workers and a police officer gave the fear of getting infected as their reason for not visiting the home.

ACTIVITY 6.4

Reread the above case study about the Victoria Climbié case and make a note of your reaction to it. Perhaps you can discuss with a colleague or fellow student what you both feel and whether you both have the same feelings and emotions about the case.

Now note down your answers to the following questions;

- In the last ten months of Victoria's life the family was always on the move. How did this contribute to the organisational dangerousness exhibited in this case?

- What were your feelings after reflecting on this case? No doubt, even at this remove, we all feel a sense of shock and horror at what happened to Victoria. Yet our feelings would not be as intense as for those individuals (doctors, nurses, social workers) who witnessed her predicament at first hand and yet failed to act. Why do you think they never acted?

- On reflection, how might the effects of this aspect of professional dangerousness be lessened in the future?

- *A key part of the professional dangerousness in this case was the failure of social workers to visit the family and to communicate with Victoria on her own. One reason for this may have been their reluctance to visit the family due to feelings of intimidation and also distaste for the conditions. On reflection, what strategies do you think they or their employers could have adopted so as to minimise this danger?*

- *What lessons were you able to learn from reflecting on this case and how could you incorporate them into your future practice? Compare your answers with your colleague or fellow student. Did you both have similar answers?*

Comment

This was a clear instance of professional dangerousness, both on the part of those professionals who were directly charged with protecting her and the organisations within which they worked, and should help us to appreciate the importance of reflecting on its effects in our own practice to avoid anything similar happening again.

CHAPTER SUMMARY

In conclusion I want to draw together some of the main practical suggestions that will assist you in trying to avoid the effects of professional dangerousness when you reflect on your practice.

- When reflecting-before-action – before every visit to a family you should find out as much as you can by reviewing the case notes and discussions with colleagues. When planning for your encounter you should track down any related research tied to the reason for your visit to help you to plan your strategy. Be aware of the way your own reaction to any hostile behaviour can prevent you from carrying out a proper assessment of the situation within the family.

- When reflecting-in-action – while interviewing a family with regard to child protection, try not to mirror any observed aggressive behaviour in your dealings with the carers and set out the non-negotiable areas (such as seeing the child on its own) at an early stage in the relationship.

- Always set aside some time for reflecting-on-action – reviewing features of the case after the visit, to allow you to learn future strategies that will allow you to avoid, or at least minimise, the effects of the problems associated with professional dangerousness. This could include a change in direction of your intervention, such as in the Climbié case, to alter it from child in need to child protection.

- Finally, think 'outside the box' so you can see in what ways the culture of the organisation you work within may work so as to enhance professional dangerousness rather than inhibit it and try to compensate for this in dealing with your cases. Ticking the latest government inspired boxes is at best an *aide mémoire* and is not a substitute for good practice.

FURTHER READING

Koprowska, J (2005) *Communication and interpersonal skills in social work.* Exeter: Learning Matters.

Chapter 9 of this book will help you to recognise some of the clues that point to likely aggressive behaviour.

Braithwaite, R (2001) *Managing aggression.* London: Routledge.

This is a useful guide to strategies for managing aggression.

REFERENCES

Braithwaite, R (2001) *Managing aggression*. London: Routledge.

Department of Education (2010) Building a safe and confident future – implementing the recommendations of the Social Work Task Force. Available at: www.education.gov.uk/publications/standard/publicationdetailpage1/

Ferguson, H (2005) Working with violence, the emotions and the psycho-social dynamics of child protection: reflections on the Victoria Climbié Case. *Social Work Education*, 24(7): 781–95.

Ferguson, H and O'Reilly, M (2001) *Keeping children safe: Child abuse, child protection and the promotion of welfare*. Dublin: A&A Farmer.

Forrester, D, McCambridge, J, Waissbein, C and Rollnick, S (2008) How do child and family social workers talk to parents about child welfare concerns? *Child Abuse Review*, 17: 23–35.

Gould, N and Baldwin, M (2004) *Social work, critical reflection and learning organization*. Aldershot: Ashgate.

Howe, D (1995) *Attachment theory for social work practice*. Basingstoke: Palgrave Macmillan.

Koprowska, J (2005) *Communication and interpersonal skills in social work*. Exeter: Learning Matters.

Laming, Lord (2003) *The Victoria Climbié Inquiry*. London: The Stationery Office.

Munro, E (2011) *The Munro Review of Child Protection: Final Report – A child-centred system*. London: The Stationery Office.

Reder, P and Duncan, S (1999) *Lost innocents: A follow-up study of fatal child abuse*. London: Routledge.

Ruch, G (2002) From triangle to spiral: reflective practice in social work education, practice and research. *Social Work Education*, 21(2): 199–216.

Rustin, M (2005) Conceptual analysis of critical moments in Victoria Climbié's life. *Child and Family Social Work*, 10: 11–19.

Schön, D (1991) *The reflective practitioner: How professionals think in action*. Aldershot: Ashgate.

Thompson, N (2009) *Understanding social work: Preparing for practice*, 3rd edition. Basingstoke: Palgrave Macmillan.

Wallis, S (2004) *Developing research-informed practice in child care social work teams*. Durham: University of Durham unpublished PhD Research thesis (available online).

Chapter 7

'Doing gender' in social work practice

Chris Smethurst

Introduction

This chapter will encourage you to reflect upon the impact of gender on your practice as a qualified or student social worker. Specifically, it will enable you to explore how your identity may influence your behaviour and attitudes in practice. It will highlight the extent to which your practice is influenced by others' gendered expectations of what roles and behaviours are appropriate for you. The following activity requires you to reflect upon your own experiences of being a male or female social work student or practitioner.

ACTIVITY **7.1**

To what extent do you think your gender has had an impact upon the following:

Your choice of career?

The roles and behaviours that are expected of you in the workplace?

What do we mean when we talk about 'gender'?

'Gender' is often used interchangeably with 'sex' when referring to the distinction between men and women. However, 'sex' seems to imply distinctions based upon biological difference, whereas 'gender' can be understood more in terms of the individual's personal identity. This identity can incorporate physical characteristics, but may be influenced by practices and expectations that are culturally determined. Oakley (1979) explores the extent to which 'gender' can be viewed in terms of learnt behaviour linked to social expectations. Social learning theories are particularly useful in enabling us to understand how individuals learn and internalise the 'gender rules' of masculinity and femininity. Individuals may learn to define themselves in relation to the characteristics and behaviours that are deemed to be 'typical' or 'appropriate' for men or women: 'masculine' and 'feminine' respectively. At one level, these characteristics might seem obvious; you can probably immediately conjure up an image of a 'masculine' man or a 'feminine' woman. However, you might consider the extent to which your characterisations are merely stereotypes; or, perhaps, represent polar opposites on a continuum.

ACTIVITY **7.2**

From the following list of roles and characteristics, note down which you would classify as being associated with masculinity and which with femininity: physically strong, decisive, assertive, caring, loving, commanding, sensitive, aggressive, emotionally detached, nurturing, empathic, dynamic, rational, provider, breadwinner, home-maker, violent, dominant, competitive, sensual, risk-taker, stoic, tough, a people person, independent, entrepreneurial, a good listener, giving, values relationships, reflective, takes charge.

Comment

You may have discovered that it was relatively easy to clearly define some of the characteristics as being stereotypically masculine or feminine. However, maybe some of the characteristics could apply to both genders; or increasingly be viewed as non-gender specific. This is not surprising if we accept that masculine and feminine roles and behaviour are less clearly defined than they might have been in the past; and are not merely determined by biological difference. It is beyond the scope of this chapter to provide an in-depth discussion of these issues; however, Butler (2004) provides a useful collection of essays which transcend a conception of gender as in binary terms and as biologically determined. Similarly, within social work, it is important to recognise that gender cannot be considered without reference to power and the extent to which 'the masculine' and 'the feminine' are afforded value and status (Hicks, 2015).

Making sense of gender as a social construction

As a social work student, you will have encountered discussions of gender in relation to anti-oppressive practice. It is likely that you will have been asked to reflect on the impact of gender in your relationships with service users and with your colleagues and supervisors. However, when reflecting on the impact of gender in social work practice, students are confronted with a range of potentially conflicting perspectives. Nevertheless, Hicks (2015) notes that within social work, gender is often assumed to be a rather static quality, a 'given' which, in turn, can lead to a narrow conceptualisation of social problems and social work interventions. Therefore, there is a challenge in acknowledging that specific issues may be experienced very differently by men and women, while recognising that the experiences of individual men and women should not be subsumed by normative generalisations and assumptions.

MacInnes (1998) provides a useful starting point in attempting to untangle some of this complexity. He argues that although the continuing oppression of women is evident in many areas of economic and social life, the historic demarcation between men's and women's social roles, behaviours and activities has become increasingly blurred. It is proposed that collective identities, such as class and gender, are giving way to forms of identity that are far more personalised (Kumar, 1995; Bauman, 2004; Buckingham, 2008). Our aspirations play a big part in defining our personalised identity: that is, how we would like to see ourselves and how we would like others to view us.

However, we need to exercise a degree of caution when assessing the extent to which our personal identities are a matter of choice. Although there may be a blurring of boundaries between gender roles and aspirations, this is not the same as saying that differences do not exist. There is evidence that socialisation and the pressure to conform to particular roles and behaviours that we perceive are *expected* of men and women, are still powerful in defining how we *ought* to be. How we think others perceive and even *judge* us are perhaps important considerations in understanding how we learn the gender rules of behaviour. Butler explores how our gendered identities are 'performed', she uses the term 'improvised', in relation to others: *one does not 'do' one's gender alone. One is always 'doing' with or for another, even if the other is only imaginary* (2004, p1). Similarly, Butler suggests that: *Sometimes a normative conception of gender can undo one's personhood, undermining the capacity to persevere in a liveable life* (2004, p1).

These quotes certainly underline the contention that gender, despite being an individual performance or improvisation, is still subject to powerful constraint, even though this is not always immediately apparent.

Despite there being a considerable body of evidence that suggests that gender roles and identities are becoming increasingly fluid, it is perhaps surprising that biology still underpins many of the assumptions and myths about men and women (Macionis and Plummer, 2008; Furness, 2012). MacInnes (1998, p9) provides a neat summary of this apparent paradox: *We increasingly acknowledge the equal rights of women and men, but cling to the conviction that the different sexes of our bodies contain the key to other, more fundamental distinctions.*

Interestingly, recent advances in neuro-science and genetics appear to provide further evidence that men and women are essentially 'different'. This in turn has fuelled an apparent resurgence of interest in biological determinism as a means of understanding social behaviour. However, scientific authority is not the only factor supporting this renewed interest: Sennett (2004) argues that a frequent societal response to economic and social insecurity is to look for an attractive, if illusory, degree of certainty in an uncertain world. However, this does not refute the science, which is often cited as 'proving' an underlying biological blueprint for social norms. Fine (2010) provides a useful critique of this biological determinism; but, for our purposes, it is perhaps worth homing in on one of the most popular contemporary topics: the differences between the male and female brain. It is undoubtedly the case that these differences exist and have a powerful influence; however, Kimura (1999) notes that the differences between the genders can be less than the differences between individuals of the same gender.

Perhaps the best conclusion we can come to is that the construction of gender identity, for each individual, is subject to the operation and interaction of a complex array of variables. Some of these variables are biological, some may be specific to individual life experiences and some may link to cultural norms. Additionally, the 'performance' of gender may be contextual; for example, is an individual's gender performance different at work from how it is at home? Furthermore, the study of 'intersectionality' (Crenshaw, 1989) illustrates the interaction of gender, race, class, sexuality, age and religion to provide a more nuanced understanding of individual identity; particularly, in relation to advantage, discrimination and oppression.

Free to be the person we want to be?

Pressure to conform to a particular notion of femininity has been highlighted by a number of authors. They have argued that there is a societal expectation that women will care for others; this involves both physical labour and emotional investment (Finch and Groves, 1983; Graham, 1983; Folbre, 2001). These external expectations derive not only from women's biological identities as mothers, but from a social construction of femininity that values women who are nurturing, caring and self-sacrificing. These images provide a powerful message to women about what is 'appropriate' feminine behaviour. Arguably, there has been considerable evolution in the demarcation of gender roles and expectation since the research of the early 1980s. However, contemporary sources suggest that the gendered division of caring responsibilities has remained remarkably static (Himmelweit, 2008).

In fact, it has been suggested that there has been a resurgence of social conservatism that is resistant to change and reinforces stereotypical gender roles (Folbre, 2001; Webb and Childs, 2012).

Arguably, men are not immune from gender stereotyping and have particular templates of what a man *should be*. Defining characteristics of masculinity have been identified by Bowl (2001) and can be summarised as: being successful in the role of breadwinner, provider and father; appearing to be strong, competent, decisive, assertive and independent; maintaining control of one's emotions to maintain the impression of being logical and rational.

Connell (2000; Connell and Messerschmidt, 2005) acknowledges that not all men conform to a particular image of the idealised man; nor do all men wish to define themselves according to a fixed notion of what a man should aspire to be. However, Connell coins the term 'hegemonic masculinity', which recognises that although there may be many ways of defining and being masculine, a dominant image of masculinity still exists that provides an aspirational template of how men are expected to be. Therefore, physical strength, heterosexuality, independence and the suppression of emotion and vulnerability are still presented in popular culture as idealised and valued masculine traits; against these, men can be compared and found wanting. Gay men, men who are nurturing and emotionally sensitive, men who do not conform to the idealised form of masculinity, can still be masculine but they are at risk of being labelled as not being 'real men'. Similarly, hegemonic masculinity recognises that gender identity is not divorced from the issue of social power: hegemonic masculinity dominates all constructions of femininity and *subordinate masculinities*.

ACTIVITY 7.3

List the roles, behaviours and characteristics that you think you are expected to adopt as a social worker because you are either a man or a woman.

* *Which ones do you strongly identify with?*
* *Are there some that you reject?*

Gender roles in social work practice

Hood et al. (1998) illustrate the extent to which women were perceived to bring to post-war British social work special qualities that were viewed as being essentially feminine: the ability to engage with others and to set both children and adults at their ease (Curtis Report, 1946, para. 446). Empathy, sensitivity and the ability to read and manage others' emotions are skills and qualities typically associated with women. Hochschild (1983) argues that women's greater facility with emotion is a valued and essential characteristic of occupations where women predominate; in fact, it should be recognised as being emotional labour. Gorman and Postle (2003) suggest that emotional labour is integral to good social work practice, but because it is seen as something women do naturally it is often unrecognised or undervalued by social work agencies. Instead, greater value is often afforded to processes and qualities that are perceived as essentially masculine: managerial skills, the ability to remain emotionally detached, or technical skills with IT or administrative systems.

Approximately 87 per cent of UK social workers are female and only 13.6 per cent of students on social work courses are male (GSCC, 2010; Ashencaen Crabtree and Parker, 2014). Consequently, a number of authors have speculated as to whether social work is an unusual or non-traditional occupation for men (Williams, 1995; Christie, 1998). Nevertheless, there is a great deal of empirical evidence that despite their minority status men enjoy gender privilege in relation to their career prospects: men may quickly ascend the 'glass elevator' of promotion to higher status management positions and are statistically over-represented in senior positions (McPhail, 2004; Lazzari et al., 2009).

Research by Shen-Miller et al. (2011) suggests that within non-traditional occupations men do internalise expectations of how they ought to behave as men. These behaviours were often reflected in 'traditional' masculine responses to situations that were emotive (for example, that men confront danger or remain calm in challenging situations). The researchers conclude that this limited the scope of the men's work and reinforced stereotypical constructions of masculinity in the workplace. These themes are explored in the following case study.

CASE STUDY

Luke is a social worker in a local authority children and families team. He qualified two years ago and has worked in this team since qualifying. He is the only man in the team and the longest-serving team member, with the exception of his team manager and the senior practitioner. Luke enjoys what he calls the 'buzz' that he gets from his work but finds that he sometimes feels stressed and out of his depth. However, he is always reliable and never lets anyone down. He feels quite pleased that other members of the team respect him and ask his advice. Luke thinks that he frequently gets allocated to work with difficult service users, particularly men. His manager often asks him to accompany female workers on their visits to potentially aggressive clients. Luke thinks that he has learnt a lot from watching how his female colleagues defuse certain situations but he also thinks that they appreciate his support in a crisis. Luke hopes that he can act as a role model to young male service users to show them that men can be caring and sensitive, but still be men.

ACTIVITY 7.4

Considering the case study, can you identify the risks for Luke?

Comment

The characteristics of stereotypical forms of masculinity might enable us to under-stand some of Luke's experiences. For example, we could question how easy it would be for Luke to admit when he was feeling stressed or out of his depth. This could be particularly problematic, as Luke seems to value the status he receives from being seen as capable and reliable. This may, of course, pose some risks for Luke and maybe for service users and colleagues too. Other risks may be identified in the apparent expectation that Luke's gender equips him to deal with difficult or aggressive clients. Perhaps Luke and his manager might reflect on what exactly Luke is expected to do and be in these situations. If Luke aspires to be a role model, perhaps he may also consider the possible contradictions in the roles expected of him.

RESEARCH SUMMARY

Simpson (2004) explores the experiences of men in female majority occupations. Her findings suggest the following:

- *Women may not receive the same career development opportunities as their male colleagues who may be fast-tracked or groomed for promotion by receiving enhanced training.*

- *Men may receive special consideration from female colleagues. This can include the dubious benefits of being 'mothered', but may also include being treated more leniently by female managers.*

- *Men may experience the assumed authority effect: masculine status resulting in deference from colleagues and other professionals and an assumption of competence and expertise.*

- *The assumption of competence can place men in professional situations that their knowledge and experience does not equip them to deal with.*

Simpson (2004) provides a useful insight into the way men and women interact in organisations. It would appear that even in occupations where their numbers dominate, women experience considerable disadvantage compared to their male col-leagues. However, men in female majority occupations do experience some negativity. Hicks (2001) suggests that male social workers may indeed be perceived as 'nice' and 'caring' men; but they risk being characterised as 'soft' or 'effeminate'. In addition, men in direct care work with children may be viewed with suspicion.

Women moving into the male-dominated world of management may be viewed with suspicion and hostility. However, such hostility may originate from their colleagues, both male and female. To adapt to the dominant organisational culture women may, through choice or necessity, adopt behaviours that are associated with mascu-linity, such as toughness and emotional detachment (Kerfoot, 2001). However, this appears to be something of a 'double-edged sword', with women who display these characteristics frequently being perceived negatively by male and female colleagues

(Eagly and Carli, 2007; Heilman and Okimoto, 2007). Nevertheless, it is perhaps of particular concern that a number of studies have suggested that in order to be seen as capable and suitable for promotion women must suppress emotional displays because these could be viewed as a sign of weakness. For men, too, it would appear that being 'professional' is associated with the suppression and denial of emotion. These implications will be explored in the next section.

Gender and the emotional impact of social work

In Chapter 3 Gill Butler highlights the need for practitioners to be able to reflect upon their own and others' emotions and argues that emotional intelligence is an integral part of effective social work practice. The value base of social work draws heavily upon notions of caring, nurturing and emotional support, but there is an additional expectation that social workers will engage in distressing and emotionally challenging situations. Research has revealed the incidence of anxiety, fear and emotional distress in social work practice; yet recognition and support within agencies is variable (Smith, 2005; Ferguson, 2011). The failure to acknowledge the emotional aspects of the work is convincingly addressed by Ferguson (2005, 2011) and summarised in Sandra Wallis' chapter on professional dangerousness (see Chapter 6).

ACTIVITY 7.5

Consider an experience at work or on placement that was emotionally challenging.

- *What did you feel at the time?*

- *Did you get any support at work? From whom?*

Comment

Smith (2005) demonstrates that the support of colleagues, including the line manager, is key to enabling social workers to deal with the anxiety and distress that they may encounter through their job. Failure to acknowledge and address the emotional impact of work can result in emotional 'burn-out' (Hochschild, 1983) or lead to dangerous practice (Ferguson, 2005, 2011). In the past eight years, there has been a rapid expansion of interest and research concerning resilience and social workers. However, it is perhaps surprising that consideration of gender is largely absent from the research. Although it does not specifically address gender, the following research summary explores the connection between emotional resilience and the lived experience and personal identity of social work students. Consequently, it is relevant to the themes discussed in this chapter. Particularly, the study highlights that social work students who were interviewed equated the expression of emotion with being unprofessional.

RESEARCH SUMMARY

Focusing on resilience and personal identity, Rajan-Rankin (2013) conducted semi-structured interviews with ten undergraduate social work students. The research highlighted the following themes:

- *Students experienced discomfort, to a greater or lesser degree, in dealing with emotion during their course. Emotional containment was seen as important and the study highlighted the tensions between the expression of emotion and perceived notions of professionalism.*

- *Social support was perceived as essential for coping with stress. The importance of informal networks, as well as formal supervision, was highlighted.*

- *Identity and difference were explored, with some students feeling that it was not safe to be themselves. The study did not focus on gender but upon race, religion and sexuality.*

CASE STUDY

Julie is a social work student on placement. She has been working with a 15-year-old young person called Dan, who has a history of offending behaviour. Teachers and other social workers perceive Dan as being uncommunicative and aggressive and Julie acknowledges that Dan's behaviour has often left her feeling anxious, frustrated and irritated. However, she tries not to show this in her work with Dan, not least because she feels that he may be trying to 'wind her up' and she does not want to give him the satisfaction of knowing that he is irritating her. In supervision, Julie has recognised that some of her frustration stems from feeling that she is 'not getting through to Dan'. Because this makes Julie doubt her own competence, she feels angry towards Dan. Julie acknowledges that her reactions are unprofessional and resolves not to let Dan upset her. She secretly acknowledges that she feels intimidated by many of the young male service users she works with but strives hard to ensure that she does not demonstrate any vulnerability.

Julie learned that Dan had been in a fight outside school, where he was attacked by a group of young people. The teacher Julie spoke to suggested that Dan had been 'winding people up, like he usually does' but Dan would not say anything about what had happened. Julie visited Dan and asked him to describe what occurred. Dan started to speak, then began to cry. Julie was surprised because Dan had always seemed so combative and she had not expected him to cry. Dan quickly got embarrassed and said he was 'OK', and that he did not want to talk about the incident. Julie changed the subject, then immediately regretted doing so.

ACTIVITY 7.6

Place yourself in Julie's position; what would you do next?

Comment

The case study illustrates a familiar question for social workers: how to respond to someone who is distressed. In this situation, Dan appears to have become embarrassed about crying in front of Julie. You might consider whether Julie was right not to explore the cause of Dan's distress. If you do not think she was right, what could she have done differently? You might reflect on whether it would have been easier, or more difficult, for both participants if they had been female; or if both had been male. Similarly, you may wish to explore whether some of Julie's apprehension may have stemmed from stereotypical assumptions about masculinity and male service users. Within social work, masculinity and male service users are frequently perceived as threatening, worthless or problematic (Christie, 2001; Scourfield, 2006). Alternatively, you may wish to consider whether Julie's feelings of anxiety are illustrative of the inherently problematic nature of masculinity, as demonstrated by Dan's behaviour towards her and others. You need to consider whether the behaviour and attitudes of Julie and Dan have any consequences for their longer-term emotional resilience.

Reflecting on gender in social work training

Within social work, feminist perspectives have been particularly effective in ensuring that qualified social workers are aware of the discrimination and disadvantage that many women experience. Similarly, throughout their careers, it is likely that social workers will encounter the consequences of abuse, violence and criminal activity; the overwhelming majority of this behaviour will be perpetrated by men. Therefore, it is unsurprising that a considerable body of literature has explored the links between a range of social problems and the nature of 'masculinity'. In essence, this literature highlights the problems that men cause and asks whether there is something specifically problematic with male biology, psychology and socialisation. These debates are not confined to academia: a recent best-selling popular psychology book is entitled *The problem with women is ... men* (Orlando, 2008).

Orlando's book is not mentioned in order to trivialise important issues, but to illustrate a further consideration: the extent to which discussion of gender can be impeded by polarisation and defensiveness. Arguably, the issue of gender in social work training has tended to focus on women's experiences; specifically, those of discrimination and disadvantage. Men largely feature as sources of problems, either through their individual behaviour or because of the structural advantages they experience in a male-dominated society. Perhaps it is worth stressing that the influence of gender is not, inevitably, female-centric. Similarly, there are risks in assuming that structural advantages are equally distributed, that men and women are homogenous groups and that individual men and women are representative of, and responsible for, their gender group. Within an educational setting, these risks are illustrated by Gough (2001) who notes that many male students felt the need to 'defend' their gender or 'bite their tongue' during gender-related discussion. Similarly, Ashencaen Crabtree and Parker (2014) reveal that male students occupy a vulnerable position that oscillates between privilege and marginalisation and the experience of sexism.

Feelings of 'guilt' are arguably a consistent but under-analysed feature of social work training: specifically, whether feeling guilty is either appropriate or useful for practice. Lloyd and Degenhardt (2000) advocate directly challenging male students to take responsibility for the behaviour of their gender. However, this raises the question of whether or not a male social worker is somehow implicated in the violence and abuse perpetrated by male social work clients. Similarly, is it problematic to note that the majority of aggressive acts are committed by men and thus conclude that men, *all men*, are aggressive? Arguably, there is a risk in confusing correlation with causation: as Hicks (2015, p473) points out, the majority of abuse may be committed by one gender, but does this show that gender *causes* abuse?

One of the key challenges for any social worker, whatever their level of experience, is to be able to conceptualise highly complex situations, often based upon limited and sometimes contradictory information. This creates a risk of interpreting what we see through our own lens of perception; in other words, our preferred theories or prejudices. Psychologists refer to this as 'anchoring bias', in that we anchor our interpretation to what we already know. Similarly, 'confirmation bias' leads us to privilege or look for evidence that supports our preconceived ideas.

The range of perspectives concerning gender is both confusing and emotive and this may prove problematic when searching for some certainty in relating theory to practice. Arguably, our understanding of the process of reflection should enable us in these considerations. The work of Schön (1983, 1987, 1992) suggests that we should be wary of attempting to uncritically apply a particular theory; or reject it, if it does not appear to correspond with our own experience. He suggests that we engage in a 'reflective conversation' where we blend our theoretical knowledge with our own personal experience to gain a greater understanding of a specific situation. Schön notes that real-life practice situations can be messy, involving uncertainty that may challenge our preconceptions and beliefs.

ACTIVITY **7.7**

Reflect upon your experience of how gender was addressed in your social work training.

- *Recall one specific session or topic. How did you feel during and after the session?*
- *In what ways did it inform your understanding of practice?*
- *Were there any aspects of this session that were unsuccessful? Why do you think it was unsuccessful?*

CASE STUDY

Lynn is in her late forties and has embarked on social work training, having spent the last 15 years raising a family. She is now in her second year at university and has been pleasantly surprised at how well she has done academically. Reflecting on her own

(Continued)

experiences of school, she realises that she did not fulfil her potential. Although her brother went to university, Lynn's parents believed that girls should not be encouraged to pursue academic or professional careers. Lynn married young but is now divorced. On reflection, she realises that her ex-husband always seemed to be threatened by her intelligence and was absolutely set against her going to college. Through talking to other women on the course, Lynn has become aware that hers is not a unique experience.

She has found that the teaching of gender issues on her course has enabled her to make sense of some of these experiences. Lynn was particularly interested to learn of the feminist perspectives on caring. She remembered that when her mother became ill, the family and other professionals seemed to expect Lynn to care for her; such an expectation did not apply to her brother. She recalls the stress and guilt that she experienced in attempting to reconcile all the conflicting demands that were placed upon her.

This chapter has provided an introduction to a number of perspectives on gender. There are some omissions: for example, the experiences of transgendered men and women. Nevertheless, you will have gained an appreciation of the complexity of the issues and the implications for you as a practitioner. In Chapter 3 Gill Butler argues that through reflection-in-action the emotionally intelligent practitioner understands what others expect from them and how to behave or react 'appropriately' in a given situation. In relation to gender, you need to consider the ways in which practitioners develop an understanding of how to react appropriately. Specifically, in social work practice, what are the benefits of conforming to how we feel we ought to behave and what are the costs if we do not?

CHAPTER SUMMARY

- The influence of gender is a key feature of social work practice; yet, the range of theory can be confusing for students seeking to apply a particular perspective to their own experiences.

- Schön (1983, 1992) provides a useful framework for acknowledging and understanding that reflective practice requires a flexible and critical approach to the application of theory to the uncertain real world of practice.

- Students could be reluctant to openly engage with and discuss some of the issues concerning gender. This may be because issues are contentious and students are anxious about 'saying the wrong thing'.

- Exploring theory and research and reflecting on your own experiences, views and behaviour will enable you to understand how gender impacts upon your own practice.

- It is beneficial to consider the emotional impact of social work and reflect upon how your gender may affect your responses to particular situations and the support you may receive from others.

Christie, A (ed.) (2001) *Men in social work*. Basingstoke: Palgrave Macmillan.

This book provides a thorough and accessible summary of relevant debates.

Clouston,TJ (2015) *Challenging stress burnout and rust-out: Finding balance in busy lives.* London: Jessica Kingsley.

Explores the challenges and pressures practitioners experience in seeking a work-life balance.

Ferguson, H (2011) *Child protection practice*. Basingstoke: Palgrave Macmillan.

This book is an essential text for those who wish to understand more about the role of emotion in social work practice.

Smith, M (2005) *Surviving fears in health and social care: The terrors of night and the arrows of day*. London: Jessica Kingsley.

Ashencaen Crabtree, S and Parker, J (2014) Being male in female spaces: perceptions of male students on masculinity on a qualifying course. *Revista de Asisten   Social* , XIII (4): 7–26.

Bauman, Z (2004) *Identity*. Cambridge: Polity.

Bowl, R (2001) Men and community care. In A Christie (ed.), *Men in social work*. Basingstoke: Palgrave Macmillan.

Buckingham, D (2008) Introducing identity. In D Buckingham and CT MacArthur (eds), *Youth, identity, and digital media*. Cambridge, MA: MIT Press.

Butler, J (2004) *Undoing gender*. London Routledge

Christie, A (1998) Is social work a non-traditional occupation for men? *British Journal of Social Work*, 28: 491–510.

Christie, A (ed.) (2001) *Men and social work: Theories and practices*. Basingstoke: Palgrave Macmillan.

Connell, R (2000) *The men and the boys*. Cambridge: Polity.

Connell, R and Messerschmidt, J (2005) Hegemonic masculinity: rethinking the concept. *Gender and Society*, 19(6): 829–59.

Crenshaw, K (1989) Demarginalizing the intersection of race and sex: a black feminist critique of antidiscrimination doctrine, feminist theory and antiracist politics. *University of Chicago. Legal Forum*, 139.

Curtis Report (1946) *Care of children: Inter-department committee report*, Curtis Committee, Cmd 6922. London: HMSO.

Eagly, A and Carli, L (2007) Women and the labyrinth of leadership. *Harvard Business Review*, 85(9): 63–71.

Ferguson, H (2005) Working with violence, the emotions and the psycho-social dynamics of child protection: reflections on the Victoria Climbié case. *Social Work Education*, 24(7): 781–95.

Ferguson, H (2011) *Child protection practice*. Basingstoke: Palgrave Macmillan.

Ferguson, I (2008) *Reclaiming social work: Challenging neoliberalism and promoting social justice*. London: Sage.

Finch, J and Groves, D (1983) *A labour of love: Women, work and caring*. London: Routledge and Kegan Paul.

Fine, C (2010) *Delusions of gender: The real science behind sex differences*. London: Icon.

Folbre, N (2001) *The invisible heart: Economics and family values*. New York: New Press.

Furness, S (2012) Gender at work: characteristics of 'failing' social work students. *British Journal of Social Work*, 42: 480–99.

General Social Care Council (2010) *Raising standards: Social work education in England 2008–09,* London: GSCC.

Gorman, H and Postle, K (2003) *Transforming community care: A distorted vision*. Birmingham: Venture Press.

Gough, B (2001) Biting your tongue: negotiating masculinities in contemporary Britain. *Journal of Gender Studies*, 10(2): 169–85.

Graham, H (1983) Caring: a labour of love. In J Finch and D Groves (eds), *A labour of love: Women, work and caring*. London: Routledge and Kegan Paul.

Heilman, ME and Okimoto, TG (2007) Why are women penalized for success at male tasks? The implied communality effect. *Journal of Applied Psychology*, 92(1): 81–92.

Hicks, S (2001) Men social workers in children's services: 'Will the real man please stand up?' In A Christie (ed.), *Men in social work*. Basingstoke: Palgrave Macmillan.

Hicks, S (2015) Social work and gender: an argument for practical accounts. *Qualitative Social Work*, 14(4): 471–87.

Himmelweit, S (2008) *Reducing gender inequalities to create a sustainable care system*. York: Joseph Rowntree Foundation.

Hochschild, A (1983) *The managed heart: Commercialization of human feeling*. Berkeley, CA: University of California Press.

Hood, P, Everitt, A and Runnicles, D (1998) Femininity, sexuality and professionalism in the children's departments. *British Journal of Social Work*, 28(4): 471–90.

Kerfoot, D (2001) The organization of intimacy: managerialism, masculinity and the masculine subject. In SM Whitehead and FJ Barrett (eds), *The masculinities reader*. London: Cambridge Press.

Kimura, D (1999) *Sex and Cognition*. Cambridge MA: MIT Press.

Kumar, K (1995) *From post-industrial to post-modern society*. Oxford: Basil Blackwell.

Lazzari, MM, Colarossi, L and Collins, KS (2009) Feminists in social work: where have all the leaders gone? *Affilia: Journal of Women and Social Work*, 24: 348–59.

Lloyd, S and Degenhardt, D (2000) Challenges in working with male social work students. In K Cavanagh and VE Cree (eds), *Working with men: Feminism and social work*. London: Routledge.

MacInnes, J (1998) *The end of masculinity*. Buckingham: Open University Press.

Macionis, J and Plummer, K (2008) *Sociology*. Harlow: Pearson Education.

McPhail, BA (2004) Setting the record straight: social work is not a female-dominated profession. *Social Work*, 49(2): 323–6.

Oakley, A (1979) *Becoming a mother*. Oxford: Martin Robertson.

Orlando, CJ (2008) *The problem with women is … men.* North Charleston, SC: Booksurge Publishing.

Rajan-Rankin, S (2013) Self-identity, embodiment and the development of emotional resilience. *British Journal of Social Work*, 44(8): 2426–42.

Schön, D (1983) *The reflective practitioner: How professionals think in action*. New York: Basic Books.

Schön, D (1987) *Educating the reflective practitioner*. San Francisco: Jossey-Bass.

Schön, D (1992) Designing as reflective conversation with the materials of a design situation. *Knowledge-Based Systems*, 5(1): 3–14.

Scourfield, JB (2006) Placing gender in social work: the local and national dimensions of gender relations. *Social Work Education*, 25(7): 665–79.

Sennett, R (2004) *Respect: The formation of character in an age of equality.* London: Allen Lane.

Shen-Miller, DS, Olson, D and Boling, T (2011) Masculinity in nontraditional occupations: ecological constructions. *American Journal of Men's Health*, 5(1): 18–29.

Simpson, R (2004) Masculinity at work: the experiences of men in female dominated professions. *Work, Employment and Society*, 18(2): 349–68.

Smith, M (2005) *Surviving fears in health and social care: The terrors of night and the arrows of day.* London: Jessica Kingsley.

Webb, P and Childs, C (2012) Gender politics and conservatism: the view from the British Conservative Party grassroots. *Government and Opposition*, 47(1): 21–48.

Williams, C (1995) *Still a man's world: Men who do women's work.* Berkeley, CA: University of California Press.

Chapter 8

Reflective practice on placement

Terry Scragg

Introduction

The purpose of this chapter is to explore the use of reflective practice while you are on placement as part of your social work degree programme. Discussion of the origins of reflective practice, its evolution and relevance to social work are discussed in other chapters in this book. This chapter describes a range of practical activities that can increase your engagement with reflective practice, which will enhance your learning during your placement.

As your course progresses your knowledge and understanding of the use of reflective practice will increase and you should become more confident in recognising how you can apply the skills of reflection to different practice situations. When you begin your first placement you may find that your reflection is mainly at a descriptive level, but as you advance through your placements you are increasingly able to use reflection to analyse your practice, culminating in your final placement where you are able to reflect in a critical or transformational way. Once you are qualified as a social worker you will find reflective practice continues to play an important part in your continuing professional development, and you will be assessed in practice to gain a post-qualifying award and as part of the assessed and supported year in employment

(ASYE) (www.skillsforcare.org.uk) and the employer's standards for social workers (www.local.gov.uk/workforce). The opportunity to develop your skills in reflection while a student on placement can help you to value the importance of this activity throughout your professional career (Roulston et al., 2014).

Although this chapter is primarily concerned with the student's understanding and development of reflective practice, it should also be of interest to practice educators. The practice educator's focus on supporting the student to develop their skills in reflection is mirrored in their own need to *reflect on their own practice, monitoring and analysing the outcomes of their reflection so that new learning can be identified and shared with the student and others* (Ixer, 2003).

Reflection within the placement setting

Throughout your placements you will use a variety of approaches to develop your reflective practice. The important element in the process is that it takes place within a relationship where your practice educator can facilitate your learning through regularly reviewing your work with service users, challenging you to describe your practice, giving you feedback, and identifying your future learning needs. The main context for this to happen is the supervision session where you meet with your practice educator. To create the right conditions for reflection your practice educator needs to be familiar with your practice, understand the main social work theories relevant to your particular agency setting, and the processes involved in reflective practice. For supervision to be effective it relies critically on the quality of the relationship between practice educator and student, and is undertaken on a regular basis where there is sufficient time in an appropriate setting and in conditions of privacy and without interruptions. The practice educator also needs to be able to ask the right questions that will help you analyse your practice in a way that leads to greater insight and understanding of your actions, and those of others. You should not expect your practice educator to have all the answers to practice issues, but rather to be able to facilitate an increased awareness of the range and possible approaches that you can test out in the future.

ACTIVITY **8.1**

What is your experience of supervision?

- *Do you feel supported and is there mutual respect between you and your practice educator?*
- *Are you happy with the frequency of supervision sessions?*
- *Are you happy with the way the sessions are organised?*
- *Are you able to contribute to the agenda?*
- *Are you making a substantial contribution or always leaving it to your practice educator to take the initiative?*
- *Do you receive a copy of the supervision record following each session?*
- *Are there changes that would make the sessions more effective for you?*

Comment

Your response to these questions will indicate whether you are satisfied with the supervision arrangements, and that you feel confident that supervision takes place within a supportive and trusting relationship, where your practice educator offers non-judgemental feedback on your practice and that you feel 'safe' to disclose your anxieties or concerns about practice situations within supervision (Ixer, 2003). Where you have concerns you should discuss these with your practice educator and work together to identify how the supervision arrangement can be changed to meet your needs, and also ensure that they meet the requirements placed on the practice educator as part of their contractual agreement with the university.

RESEARCH SUMMARY

A study by Roulston et al. (2014) found that students valued supervision in a safe and supportive environment where they had a positive working relationship with their practice educator that was conducive to learning. Approachable and supportive practice educators, who also demonstrated their experience and commitment to the role, were valued by students and were influential in helping the student to develop professionally. Students also valued constructive feedback on their practice dilemmas, discussion of their feelings and values, with time to reflect on their practice. The findings of this research suggest that the quality of the supervisory relationship is a key influence on the student's learning and level of satisfaction with the placement.

Being prepared for supervision

You can increase the potential for satisfactory supervision sessions if you ensure that you are prepared in advance.

- Make notes before the session of any issues or activities that you have been involved in since the last session (in addition to your reflective journal extracts) that you want to discuss. Share this with your practice educator prior to the session, so they are prepared to discuss the issues you want to raise. You could email it along with any journal extracts you are providing for your practice educator.

- Ask your practice educator to support you in dealing with difficult situations through the use of rehearsals or role play so that you are more confident when you experience the real situation.

- Supervision is a two-way process of interaction. Make an active contribution and demonstrate your commitment to developing your practice.

- Make your own supervision notes so that you have a personal record of the discussion, decisions taken and any actions suggested by your practice educator.

How reflective practice can help you during your placement

Your practice educator should ensure that there is clarity about the purpose of reflection and that it is an activity concerned with professional learning and development, that personal issues are addressed only in so far as they affect your professional practice, and that you are comfortable discussing your performance (Fook and Askeland, 2007) within carefully established boundaries (Hunt, 2001). The establishment of ground rules and boundaries early in the placement is essential, as is a supervision agreement that outlines the practicalities that can form the basis for clear expectations on your part and those of your practice educator (Maclean and Lloyd, 2008).

An important prerequisite for your understanding and confidence in the use of reflective practice is that at an early stage both you and your practice educator explore what each of you identifies as the main elements of reflective practice and how and when it is used during the placement, recognising that it is one element among a range of potential learning opportunities. It is likely that during the first placement your understanding of reflective practice may still be developing, and therefore it is important to avoid the risk that you could be placed at a disadvantage because your level of understanding does not accord with that held by your practice educator (who in turn may have limited understanding). Clarity between you both on the purpose and forms of reflective practice can help avoid the potentially discriminatory element in the assessment of your practice, which could further increase the imbalance in power between you and your practice educator (Ixer, 1999).

ACTIVITY **8.2**

Both you and your practice educator should do the following.

- *Describe what you understand by the term 'reflective practice'.*
- *Compare your definitions.*
- *Agree a common understanding of reflective practice.*
- *Agree how and when you will make use of reflective practice.*

Comment

The purpose of this activity is to ensure that there is a broad understanding of what the term reflective practice means to you and your practice educator. This can help avoid some of the risks identified by Ixer (1999) and, if applied without prior exploration and agreement between the two parties, potentially place the student at a disadvantage and undermine their self-development.

Developing your reflective journal

Reflection can take a number of forms, with the most common approach being the journal (sometimes described as a diary or log), which you complete regularly throughout your placement, and selective entries are used as the basis for discussion with your practice educator. Describing your reactions to practice experiences is helpful in enabling you to clarify your thoughts and emotions, externalise your ideas and help you work out future strategies. If you use it to describe particular experiences that are significant to you, for example a critical incident or completing a process recording of an interview with a service user, it can also help you to measure your progress over the duration of a placement (Cottrell, 2003). It then has the potential to be a useful reminder of how your understanding of practice situations can change over time.

There is no right or wrong way to write up a reflective journal. Your approach will be one that is right for you, but it is helpful to go beyond pure description and incorporate your reactions, thoughts and feelings, and what you have learned and what you hoped to achieve (Parker, 2004). The following general guidelines will enable you to capture the essential elements of particular experiences and help in getting you started.

- Set aside some time each week for writing up your journal, but remember that it is advisable to write down particular experiences while they are still fresh in your memory. The longer you leave recording your thoughts after an experience the harder it becomes to recall exactly what happened and how you felt about it.

- Write your journal entries in the first person (I felt … , I thought …).

- Give yourself sufficient time to mull over your thoughts and ideas.

- Don't worry about style or presentation, as this is your personal journal.

- Describe what happened, but also ask yourself critical questions about the how, why, and what of a situation.

- What does your account tell you about your thoughts and feelings about the experience you have described?

CASE STUDY

Jack is in his first placement and has been asked by his practice educator to use an early supervision session to discuss how he can use his experiences to develop his understanding of reflective practice. Prior to this session they had compared their understanding of reflection and its application to practice. The practice educator, Sarah, suggests that he starts a reflective journal where each week he records his thoughts about events in the placement, particularly focusing on critical incidents or other occurrences that have been problematic or challenging and have significance for him, in a narrative form. She suggests that he records his reactions without attempting to overly edit his responses. The very act of writing his diary enables Jack to transform his thoughts into a narrative process that he can then use in supervision sessions. Sarah asks him to email his diary entry to her prior to their fortnightly supervision sessions, ensuring that no service user, carer or professional can be identified in his journal entries. Sarah reads Jack's journal entry before they meet and identifies questions that she wants to raise with him.

When they meet, Sarah invites Jack to select events from his journal and she uses the sessions to explore what the events meant for Jack in terms of his thoughts and feelings and what he has learned from the process. What she is doing is asking Jack to 'reflect on his reflections' in order that he develops greater insight into his own practice. As Jack is new to using reflection, his narrative is largely descriptive. Sarah understands his stage of development and progressively encourages Jack to take an increasingly analytical approach in his reflection, focusing on critical incidents, particularly those where he felt uncomfortable or where things didn't go as he had hoped. In this way he is encouraged to develop the skills that lead him to increasingly identify better understanding of his thoughts and feelings and the way this helps him to make connections with his personal assumptions about his practice. Sarah uses Schön's (1983) stages of reflection to provide a structure for the discussion. Through this process she challenges Jack to reflect on his experiences and helps him to appreciate the intuitive, emotional and analytic dimensions of social work practice (Munro, 2011).

Asking reflective questions

As you become more familiar with writing up entries in your reflective journal you could introduce the following set of questions as a starting point when you are thinking back over a practice experience that you will subsequently discuss with your practice educator.

- What was the event?

- Was it planned or unplanned?

- What exactly did I do (describe it precisely)?

- Why did I choose that particular approach?

- What social work theories seemed to be relevant to the situation?

- Did I work in an anti-oppressive way?

- How successful was I?

- Could I have dealt with the situation better?

- How could I do things differently next time?

- Has the reflection of my practice changed the way I intend to do things in the future?

Although we all at times reflect to some degree and draw conclusions from our experiences, here we are using the structure of a questioning process that can be applied routinely as part of your reflection of your practice, whether you record an experience in your journal or not. It can become part of an ongoing structured dialogue with your practice educator that goes beyond random reflections and is part of a process that helps you build knowledge and understanding about practice. Reflecting on an experience in this structured way is about learning from the process with the aim of gaining insights that help you influence your future practice.

ACTIVITY *8.3*

In order to develop your skill in writing reflectively, think back to a situation that challenged you in some way and feel free to write spontaneously whatever thoughts and feelings come into your head when you think about the situation. Through this process you are giving yourself permission to engage with your emotions and not censor your thoughts and feelings as you become aware of them when you recall an experience.

Comment

Freeing up your writing in this way can enable you to be honest about your practice, something you might not want to do when you discuss a situation with your practice educator, for fear of being judged not sufficiently 'professional'. If your relationship with your practice educator is founded on mutual respect and an openness between you then you should increasingly feel you can reveal more about your thoughts and feelings that can significantly increase your awareness of your values, attitudes and responses to practice situations. (See Chapter 2 for more ideas on developing reflective writing.)

Your reflective journal as evidence in assessment

To satisfactorily complete your placements you will need to submit a portfolio that demonstrates your achievements against the domains of the Professional Capabilities Framework. Entries in your reflective journal can provide valuable evidence of your progress throughout your placements and you should identify journal entries that demonstrate how your skills in reflecting on your practice have developed during the duration of the placement.

Different approaches to reflective practice

Although the reflective journal is described as an ideal tool to help you develop your reflective skills, other forms can include critical conversations with your practice educator, process recordings, and activities such as rehearsals and role play where you can test out different approaches to working with service users in a safe setting. You can also use the comments from your practice educator when they have observed your practice, and participation in team or multi-disciplinary meetings, where you explore your understanding of organisational systems, processes and cultures and how these influence agency practices. Trying different approaches can help you learn what works best for you and in what types of situation (Quinn, 2000). Where there seems to be some agreement among researchers is that critical incidents increase the potential for effective reflective thinking (Griffin, 2003; Lam et al., 2007). These researchers suggest that practice situations that generate anxiety, or appear perplexing to a student, have greater value in terms of practice learning.

ACTIVITY 8.4

Discuss with your practice educator the different forms that reflection can take and identify jointly what would be most helpful for your development.

Comment

It is useful to avoid concentrating too narrowly on particular forms of reflection and consider the potential range of opportunities during your placement that could form the basis for reflection that would provide you with a richer and more fulfilling experience. The reflective journal is an excellent starting point as it offers you the potential to use narrative as a method to tell your story about your reaction to events, particularly the emotions and feelings experienced from contact with service users and others. Use the journal alongside other forms of reflection or as an adjunct to other approaches.

RESEARCH SUMMARY

Research by Wilson and Kelly (2010) explored the challenges and opportunities that students identified themselves when on placement. Although there was a high level of satisfaction by students of both their academic programme and practice learning opportunities, the research nevertheless highlighted some key areas for improving the student learning experience. The researchers found that many students reported a high level of stress during their practice placements, often related to unexpected learning challenges and demands by practice educators and tutors. Students were also concerned about dealing with conflict situations and challenging behaviour. Where practice educators supported students to develop their skills through role play and rehearsal this was strongly valued by students.

Ensure that reflection is challenging

Together with your practice educator you should avoid the trap of reflection becoming a mechanical routine and used unthinkingly with a checklist approach taken to each experience or event discussed. This can result in not engaging with either critical thinking or the emotional impact of social work – creating the 'risk of navel gazing' – without the self-questioning, experiment and rehearsal for future action (Boud and Walker, 1998). It is also important to avoid reflective practice focusing exclusively on your individual practice and failing to consider the wider issues, including the practices, processes and routines that you observe in your placement agency. Finally, consider the wider social and economic policies that may play a contributory role in the problems experienced by service users and carers (Quinn, 2000).

Using an experiential learning approach

We have seen how the use of reflective questions can help you structure your thinking when you are writing up journal entries. To take things a stage further you can increase the effectiveness of reflection if you adopt ideas from experiential learning where you move beyond mere description of an experience and use the well-tested technique of the experiential learning cycle. There are a number of different models of experiential learning; all are essentially similar, asking you to describe an activity, evaluate and analyse your practice and identify possible future action. The best known are those of Kolb (1984) and Johns (2000). For the purposes of this chapter I have drawn on the Gibbs (1988) reflective cycle, which students find helpful in exploring their experiences. The value of using the experiential learning cycle is that it recognises that it is insufficient to have an experience and assume you will learn from it. Once you become familiar with using the learning cycle you can use it regularly to reflect on interventions, working through the cycle to help you identify if there is a particular stage(s) at which you experience problems.

Take as an example a first meeting with a service user where you have been asked by your practice educator to undertake an initial assessment prior to a further intervention. Use the stages in the learning cycle as you reflect back on that meeting.

- Stage 1: Description – What was the experience (what am I reflecting on)?

- Stage 2: Feelings – What were your personal thoughts and feelings during the experience?

- Stage 3: Evaluation – What went well and not so well about the experience? What made it difficult?

- Stage 4: Analysis – What sense did I make of the situation? What was really going on?

- Stage 5: Conclusion – What should or could I have done differently and what can I conclude about my way of working? Who or what might help?

- Stage 6: Action plan – What am I going to do differently in this type of situation next time? What steps do I need to take on the basis of what I have learnt? What support do I need to help me achieve change?

These questions can be built on with a greater depth of questioning as you become more skilled at reflecting on your practice and the work you undertake with service users becomes more complex and demanding. By adopting this approach your practice educator is helping you to understand that there is considerable potential for personal development and improvement in practice in using a questioning approach as an example. By consciously adopting a critical approach using the learning cycle it takes you beyond pure description to actively engaging with each stage of the cycle.

CASE STUDY

You are a student in an adult services team working with older people in the community. A referral has been received regarding Mr Brown, stating that he is in his late 70s and has suffered a cerebral haemorrhage (stroke) and has been admitted to hospital. Following medical treatment and a period of rehabilitation, he is now considered ready for discharge. You are asked by your practice educator to visit Mr Brown and undertake a needs assessment and his readiness for discharge so that community support services can be planned.

You meet Mr Brown in the hospital ward and explain that you are a student social worker and that you have come to complete an assessment so that the service can assess his need for support following discharge. You find it difficult to communicate with him as the stroke has affected his speech and he becomes tearful at times during the interview. You learn that Mr Brown has some mobility problems due to his right side being affected by the stroke. As you struggle through the needs assessment form it is clear that Mr Brown's main concern is anxiety about how he will cope when he leaves hospital as he lives alone and has no family support. Although he wants to return to his own home he will clearly need support to help him with everyday domestic tasks.

You speak to the ward sister to try to obtain more information about Mr Brown's ability to manage on his own but feel that the ward sister is primarily concerned with a date when Mr Brown can be discharged as there are pressures on beds. You mention that Mr Brown wants to return home if he can be supported, although the ward sister suggests that Mr Brown would be better suited to a residential home. You state that you are not in a position to make any commitments about his discharge and wish to consult your supervisor. You return to the office to discuss Mr Brown with your practice educator.

Comment

This case study provides an opportunity to explore a range of themes, including the consequences of stroke for an older person, the impact of a stroke on speech and mobility, changes in emotions or depression that are often consequences of this condition, and anxiety about coping in the future. There is also your reaction to working with an older person, where you experience communication problems, and where there are pressures from health professionals related to resource issues between hospitals and community services. For example:

- What were your initial thoughts about being allocated the case?
- What information would have helped you prepare better for the interview?
- Did your thinking change as you gained more information?

- What were your thoughts and feelings as the interview progressed?

- What theories could offer ideas?

- Was there anything you would do differently if you were allocated a similar case in the future?

- What does this case tell you about the pressures different services experience when resources are limited and there is pressure on professionals to suggest solutions that are not necessarily in the best interests of service users?

By using this process you will be able to develop an understanding of the issues that you face when working with service users and from this experience increasingly construct a body of informal knowledge from your practice (Parker and Bradley, 2010). It is important that you make links between theory and practice following an intervention, and also regularly start to identify particular theoretical perspectives that can help you anticipate some factors that are likely to be present in a particular case.

The contribution of social work theories

It can sometimes be difficult to identify specific theories and practice models that neatly fit when engaged with service users. The immediacy of involvement in direct practice can mean that consideration of social work theories periodically takes a back seat. We have seen in the previous case study that to fully engage in a purposeful way with a situation it is important to be well briefed and confident that your knowledge and understanding, however incomplete, provide you with some indication of what you are likely to face when you meet a service user for the first time. When you are allocated a case, do you think about what theories might offer some pointers to how you approach the meeting with the service user? From what you know of the situation, what theories seem to offer some understanding of the service user's predicament, what they might be experiencing, and what practice methods could offer a way of working effectively in the situation?

ACTIVITY **8.5**

To encourage you to think about how to apply theoretical perspectives to practice situations, Maclean and Harrison (2009, p23) offer some key statements that can help in this process.

- *What are the key aspects of the service user's identity?*

- *What are the key presenting issues?*

- *What are the key aspects of the agency context and practice?*

- *What are the key points of the work to be undertaken?*

> *Imagine that you are working with a young man with a learning disability who is moving from his parental home to live independently for the first time in supported accommodation. What theoretical perspectives and practice approaches does this case suggest that could offer a good understanding of the issues both he and his family face and how direct work with him could best meet his needs?*

Comment

A number of areas suggest themselves in this activity. He is a male, has a learning disability and wants to be independent. His parents may be anxious about whether he will be able to manage independently and whether he has the skills and confidence to live independently. What support will he need to manage successfully? Practice issues would include a needs assessment, the consideration of risk factors, care planning, identifying support for independent living skills, and working with the housing provider. Personalisation would be the main practice focus in this situation, ensuring the service user is at the centre of the process (SCIE, 2010).

Some of the above areas suggest an interaction of theory and practice that can provide ideas about how you could approach a similar situation. Ideally you want to move to a position where you recognise how theory underpins practice and practice informs theory (Thompson and Thompson, 2008), rather than relying on theories to provide ready-made solutions. As you gain experience and explore more complex practice issues you should begin to recognise where theories can offer new insights or help you make sense of experiences that at first were puzzling. In the words of Howe (2009, p2), *if you can make sense of what is going on, then you are half way towards knowing what to do*, and applying social work theories can mean that your practice is sensitive, intelligent and organised.

Integrating theory and practice

In her review of child protection, Munro (2011) describes how social workers draw on both theory and practice experience in their work and together these enable them to make assumptions based on sound judgements that can help in decision-making. Skills developed through academic studies enable them to make sense of practice situations, whereas intuition derived from repeated practice experience can lead to beliefs or 'gut feelings' about situations that provide some security when operating in a world of uncertainty.

Similarly, as you gain more experience of working with service users you will come to recognise how emotions influence each encounter and what you are experiencing emotionally when you connect with the service user and their experience. Ruch (2002) suggests that there are a range of potential sources of information available to the social worker when responding to a new situation – theories, professional and personal experience, the experience of service users and knowledge passed on by colleagues – that can all help you enter a situation with some understanding of possible outcomes.

But these are only assumptions. Even if they have proved reliable in the past, they may not account for incidents in the service user's life that you have no control over, or personal issues in your own life that affect your interactions and responses to encounters with service users. Although each situation is unique, by building up practice experience (intuitive understanding) and analytic knowledge (application of theoretical models) and exploring through reflection you will develop knowledge and skills over the duration of your placements that will enable you to practise confidently at a professional level.

CHAPTER SUMMARY

This chapter has introduced you to reflective learning in the context of your practice placement. It has identified the importance of supervision and your relationship with your practice educator and the value of working together to identify your understanding of reflective practice and how you can use this in your placements to support your learning. We have seen how you can use a range of practice opportunities to explore reflectively, and particularly the reflective journal. Case studies have provided examples of how you can develop skills in the use of a reflective journal and apply a structured approach to analyse your practice and learn from experiences and events during your placements. A case study of work with an older person provides an opportunity to explore challenging issues that offer ideas for future practice in different contexts. Finally the chapter reminds you of the importance of social work theories that should be an integral part of your practice. Combined with a growing understanding of different situations, this can enable you to develop both analytic and intuitive skills that can offer a degree of certainty when faced with future challenges. However, it is still important to appreciate that the uniqueness of each encounter suggests that a healthy scepticism is important in any practice situation.

FURTHER READING

Maclean, S and Harrison, R (2009) *Theory and practice: A straightforward guide for social work students.* Rugeley: Kirwin Maclean Associates.

A guide written by experienced practice educators that explains the major theories used in social work practice. Particularly helpful in relating theory to practice when on placement.

Howe, D (2009*) A brief introduction to social work theory.* London: Palgrave Macmillan.

This excellent introductory text describes a range of social work theories, perspectives and approaches in an accessible way, providing a helpful overview of contemporary practice.

Parker, J (2004) *Effective practice learning in social work.* London: Sage.

This book provides a comprehensive exploration of the essential components of good practice learning, such as the integration of theory, reflection, assessment and the use of supervision.

REFERENCES

Boud, D and Walker, D (1998) Promoting reflection in professional courses: the challenge of context, *Studies in Higher Education*, 23(2): 191–206.

Cottrell, S (2003) *Skills for success: The personal development planning guide.* London: Palgrave Macmillan.

Fook, J and Askeland, G (2007) Challenges of critical reflection: nothing ventured, nothing gained. *Social Work Education*, 26(5): 520–33.

Gibbs, G (1988) *Learning by doing*. Oxford: Oxford Brookes University.

Griffin, M (2003) Using critical incidents to promote and assess reflective thinking in preservice teachers. *Reflective Practice*, 4(2): 207–20.

Howe, D (2009) *A brief introduction to social work theory*. Basingstoke: Palgrave Macmillan.

Hunt, C (2001) Shifting shadows: metaphors and maps for facilitating reflective practice. *Reflective Practice*, 2(3): 257–87.

Ixer, G (1999) There's no such thing as reflection. *British Journal of Social Work*, 29(4): 513–27.

Ixer, G (2003) Developing the relationship between reflective practice and social work values. *Journal of Practice Teaching*, 5(1): 7–22.

Johns, C (2000) *Becoming a reflective practitioner*. Oxford: Blackwell.

Kolb, D (1984) *Experiential learning*. London: Prentice Hall.

Lam, C, Wong, H and Leung, T (2007) An unfinished reflexive journey: social work students reflection on their placement experiences. *British Journal of Social Work*, 37(1): 91–105.

Maclean, S, and Lloyd, I (2008) *Developing quality practice learning in social work: A straightforward guide for practice teachers and supervisors*. Rugeley: Kirwin Maclean Associates.

Maclean, S. and Harrison, R (2009) *Theory and practice: A straightforward guide for social work students*. Rugeley: Kirwin Maclean Associates.

Munro, E (2011) *The Munro review of child protection: Final Report – a child centred system*. London: Department of Education.

Parker, J (2004) *Effective practice learning in social work*. London: Sage.

Parker, J and Bradley, G (2010) *Social work practice: Assessment, planning, intervention and review*, 3rd edition. London: Sage.

Quinn, FM (2000) Reflection and reflective practice. In C Davies, L Finlay and A Bullman (eds), *Changing practice in health and social care*. London: Sage.

Roulston, A, Cleak, H and Vreugdenhil, A (2014) *Final report on model of supervision influencing student development in social work practice learning opportunities*. Available at: www.niscc.info (accessed 15 October 2015).

Ruch, G (2002) From triangle to spiral: reflective practice in social work education, practice and research. *Social Work Education*, 2: 199–216.

Schön, D (1983) *The reflective practitioner: How professionals think in action*. London: Temple Smith.

SCIE (2010) *Personalisation briefing: Implications for social workers in adults' services*. Social Care Institute for Excellence. Available at: www.scie.org.uk (accessed 6 October 2015).

Thompson, S and Thompson, N (2008) *The critically reflective practitioner*. Basingstoke: Palgrave Macmillan.

Wilson, G and Kelly, B (2010) Enhancing social work students' learning experiences and readiness to undertake practice learning. Available at: www.swap.ac.uk (accessed 11 September 2015).

Part 3
Maintaining reflective practice

Chapter 9

Working with your manager

Terry Scragg

A C H I E V I N G   A   S O C I A L   W O R K   D E G R E E

This chapter will help you to develop the following capabilities from the Professional Capabilities Framework:

- **Critical reflection and analysis** – Apply critical reflection and analysis to inform and provide a rationale for professional decision-making.
- **Context and organisations** – Engage with, inform and adapt to changing contexts that shape practice.

It will also introduce you to the following standards as set out in the 2008 social work subject benchmark statements:

2   Defining principles
3.1.5   The nature of social work practice
3.2.5   Skills in personal and professional development

Introduction

This chapter will introduce you to the world of management, particularly the work of the team manager who is the person you will come into regular contact with both as a student on placement and when newly appointed to your first social work post. Working with your manager will be one of your most significant workplace relationships and it is important that you understand the changing world of social work management, the pressures and demands placed on front line managers and how you can work effectively with your manager. For the purposes of this chapter I have assumed that your manager is also supervising your practice and that you meet regularly to discuss your work with service users as part of your social work degree programme, postgraduate award or ASYE.

The first part of the chapter will examine the role of a front-line manager, who has key responsibilities in terms of leading a team, managing resources and allocating work, and maintaining standards and supporting staff who are directly involved in providing or arranging services. The second part is concerned with how you can make best use of the knowledge and skills of your manager and what you need to do to ensure that you are getting the best from the relationship. Here we are talking about 'managing your relationship with your manager', in other words, understanding what you need to do to ensure that you are meeting your manager's needs and at the same time receive the support you need to enable you to practise effectively, develop your skills and advance your career. The third part focuses on the important work of supporting staff and those activities that enable staff to perform well, including supervision, consultation and review. All these activities have a valuable developmental function, particularly helping the newly qualified social worker to develop a critical awareness of the potential of reflective learning.

Part one: the work of the front-line manager

Front-line managers have to make the most effective use of their staff and other resources they manage. They need a clear understanding of the task and how it can be achieved, an understanding of the skills and abilities of team members, and the agency's wider resources. They also need knowledge of how the staff team can mobilise resources in the community, either through partnership with other provider organisations or by direct intervention. To achieve this they have to establish a form of work allocation and workload management that is achievable with the resources available to them to ensure that staff can manage their personal workloads without creating stress and burnout (Rosen, 2000).

Front-line managers also influence decisions due to the *positional* power invested in their role (Smith, 2010). If they are also recognised as having expertise in particular areas of social work practice they can influence decisions through *expert* power. Although power can be used *coercively* in organisations, front-line managers can use their power and influence ethically to bring about necessary changes and improvements in services.

They also have a key role in supporting, monitoring and developing social care practice. They are the 'bridge' between senior management, practitioners and service users, interpreting organisational policies and procedures, legislative requirements and practice standards to their teams (Scragg, 2009). They also play an important role in communicating and explaining senior management decisions and in turn provide information where policies and procedures are not working, and represent the opinions of front-line staff to senior management. In the words of Rosen (2000), *their job is to hold together what can seem like different worlds.*

In their research on front-line managers, Henderson and Seden (2003) argue that employers want managers to manage dilemmas, constraints and challenges which face teams at the front line of services, where they operate in situations of conflicting requirements. From an analysis of managers' job descriptions, Henderson and Seden identified the requirements of employers falling into three main functions, which were in turn identified by front-line managers who participated in their research. These are:

- Strategic – they are required to develop strategies, systems and procedures to meet the overall objectives of the service.

- Operational – they have to ensure that the service is effectively managed and that they adhere to departmental objectives and resolve operational problems.

- Professional – they have to take responsibility for managing staff, induction, supervision, training, development and appraisal. They need to ensure that all staff are empowered to undertake the tasks allocated to them, to consult them and involve them in decision-making. They also need to provide effective support and take corrective or disciplinary action where necessary.

What these three functions tell us is that front-line managers face a number of dilemmas on a regular basis. They have to focus on the operational and professional components of their role – day-to-day support and supervision of staff, allocating work, developing and enabling team members, and ensuring that they meet practice standards while at the same time responding to the demands of senior managers as part of the strategic planning process based on their local knowledge of the community their team serves. This also means that front-line managers may have to implement decisions delegated to them by senior managers that they may find personally difficult.

CASE STUDY

Sarah is a newly appointed team manager in a social work team, having been promoted from a practitioner role in the same team. Although she had a clear understanding of the work of the team manager based on her relationship with the previous post holder, she is surprised at the range and variety of demands she now has to meet in the new role. She feels comfortable working with her team colleagues and supporting their practice and maintaining relationships with a range of external organisations that work in partnership with her service, but she finds she is also expected to respond urgently to the demands of senior managers for information and to participate in strategic planning meetings, as well as manage a range of staff and financial resources within the limits set by her line manager. She now has to balance the demands of supporting and managing practice with those of strategic and resource management, including implementing decisions that she finds difficult to sell to her staff team.

ACTIVITY 9.1

When you are on placement, speak to your team manager and ask them about the demands of their role and the range of tasks they are expected to manage. Tell them you have been reading about how the management of social work has changed, for example with the emphasis on managing much tighter eligibility for services and highly constrained

(Continued)

151

financial resources, and ask them how these changes have impacted on their work as a manager. This will give you an insight into their work and help you understand the multiple pressures on them and why they have to balance the demands for services with the resources available to them.

Comment

I hope that you have now got a more informed insight into the work of a manager and understand some of the many pressures they experience stemming from their wide-ranging agenda. How your manager balances these pressures, in response to the wider demands of the organisation, and at the same time ensure that they are able to create time and space to support individual practitioners and the wider team will in the end be the test of their overall effectiveness. This places particular demands on front-line managers who are required to integrate the skills of strategic management with the knowledge and judgement of an expert practitioner.

Part two: managing your relationship with your manager

Front-line managers have a crucial role in supporting you and providing opportunities for you to engage in work-based learning through a range of practice opportunities. If you are to develop your practice from these opportunities it is important that your relationship with your manager meets your needs. Your relationship is one where you have the choice to be passive and succumb to being managed, or to develop an active approach to managing your manager. Managers do not just manage other people, they are managed themselves through the actions of their staff. Developing your skills in managing your relationship with your manager means that both of you can benefit and in turn the service becomes more effective.

Relating to your manager's world

Try to understand your manager's role, the demands on them, and how you can help them achieve their aims. Recognise that your manager is dependent on you, just as much as you are dependent on them. The following are some of the things you can do to increase your understanding of your manager.

- Be aware of the pressures and demands on your manager.

- Understand some of the constraints they work under that limit their ability to make decisions about resources that meet your recommendations.

- Understand why they may not always be available for consultation as a result of the demands on them to respond to a wide range of agendas.

- Focus on possible solutions rather than appearing to challenge their authority, so that there is a win–win outcome with the desired end obtained without you or your manager losing face.

An important part of successfully managing your relationship with your manager is your own confidence in communicating effectively and adopting an assertive approach. If you are able to communicate assertively it is more likely you will meet your own needs, but also gain the respect of your manager. In turn your manager is likely to feel more confident about your practice if they see you as a practitioner who takes your development seriously and strives to develop a relationship that is effective at both managerial and practice levels.

CASE STUDY

Paul had a positive experience of supervision while he was a student, where his practice supervisor challenged him to take increasing responsibility for his own development as he neared the end of his degree course. Now professionally qualified, he is meeting with Sarah, his team manager, to establish arrangements for supervision and the support he wants her to provide for him. He is conscious of the demands on her time, but wants to ensure that he will be able to use the supervision sessions to support his practice, to critically reflect on his interventions with clients, and also opportunities to discuss his wider professional development. In preparation for this first meeting he has spent some time identifying his own learning needs and what he would ideally like the supervision sessions to provide. In this way he is adopting a proactive approach to his own development, which will be welcomed by Sarah, who wants her team members to actively manage their own development with her support.

How you manage your relationship with your team manager will be crucial to your future development. If you can establish a relationship where you both adopt an approach that recognises the value of reflective learning and questions current practice which has become habitual or is claimed to be 'best practice', the more strategies you will develop over time that enable you to respond to the demands made on you and the service.

Actions that are likely to increase your potential for success include:

- being clear about your role and taking responsibility for your own learning;

- developing yourself to meet the demands of your practice;

- identifying your strengths and weaknesses and what you need to do to improve your practice;

- being open to changing your behaviour as a result of feedback from your manager and other colleagues;

- recognising when you need help or support and asking for it;

- giving honest and constructive feedback;

- checking when you are not clear about your manager's statements or behaviour;

- stating your own position openly, clearly expressing your thoughts and feelings.

Part three: creating a learning environment to support practice

We have seen that a particular role and function of the front-line manager is to promote and sustain practice standards through knowledge of statutory require-ments, social work standards and organisational procedures, combined with support for individual practitioners and teams through supervisory and other learn-ing activities (Kearney, 2004). The starting point for ensuring practice standards are achieved is through the manager's knowledge about how practice should be undertaken, how services are best delivered and being able and willing to share this knowledge with staff. Rosen (2000) argues that managers can best achieve this through 'modelling practice', with staff doing what managers do, rather than what they say should be done. One way this can be achieved is through managers acting as a professional consultant to the team, consulted about what could be done (methods of intervention) or what should be done (meeting statutory or pro-cedural requirements).

In order to create and sustain a culture in which continuous learning and develop-ment takes place, it is important that a manager promotes their own learning and engages in reflection on their own practice and in turn is more receptive to the development of reflection in colleagues (Thompson, 2000). The manager is in a key position to influence the development of high standards of practice. To achieve this a manager needs to understand how practice should be carried out and be up to date with knowledge-based practice developments.

The importance of the workplace as a setting for learning with the demands and challenges of practice – solving problems, improving quality or coping with change, growing out of the interaction with colleagues – is central to the notion of reflec-tive learning, with Eraut (2001) identifying the appointment and development of front-line managers as one of the most important mechanisms for promoting learning in an organisation. The appointment of front-line managers and their professional behaviour influences how staff practise; so will the standards manag-ers set for themselves. Darvill (1997), writing about work-based learning, sees this as influenced to a great extent by the manager's own style of working and how much they are seen to value this aspect of their role. He sees the front-line manager possessing influence in promoting a vision of the team and supporting a learning culture and adopting a strategic approach to the development of individuals and the team.

Ways in which managers can encourage continuous learning

Front-line managers have an important role in relation to continuous learning and should see themselves as learners. They are the most visible member of the staff team, with a complex set of roles and relationships, and therefore set an important example to other members of their team. They can facilitate staff learning through a range of activities (based on Darvill, 1997):

- declaring the importance they place on their own learning;

- actively using team meetings, supervision and case reviews as a way of asking probing questions about practice, and encouraging receptivity to new ideas;

- striking a balance between encouraging staff to take risks in testing solutions but remaining accountable for minimising risk to service users;

- encouraging staff to trust the freedom of the learning process in being open about their concerns where they feel their practice falls below their own professional standards;

- recognising that some learning may reinforce bad habits or questionable practice. Positive learning demands a willingness to question habits, to experiment and use time to reflect and develop new ways of seeing.

The front-line manager as a facilitator of workplace learning can create a climate where learning can take place. The creation of a climate for learning is seen by Thompson and Thompson (2008) as shaping the organisational culture in ways that are supportive of learning and reflection, although they recognise that you may be faced with a situation where your manager is someone who has little interest in supporting staff and sees this as a chore. Thompson and Thompson argue that if you encounter this situation you need to consider what you can do to identify those who will support you rather than accepting you have to do without learning support. If this is not possible, they suggest that you should consider whether you need to start looking for employment in a more supportive environment, as damage can be done to your morale in the short term and career in the long term in such an environment. What these comments point to is the crucial importance of organisational structures and support systems to enable the development of social work expertise.

> ### RESEARCH SUMMARY
>
> *The Chartered Institute for Personnel and Development (CIPD) training and development survey (2004) found that the three most important activities in helping employees learn effectively were the building of a culture in the organisation supportive of learning, ensuring that managers have the skills and are committed to supporting learning and development, and ensuring that employees are given time to participate in learning opportunities in the workplace. The commitment to learning at the most senior levels in*
>
> *(Continued)*

RESEARCH SUMMARY *continued*

organisations was seen as crucial in order to create a learning culture, alongside an envi-
ronment where individuals felt able to make mistakes and learn from them, and where
they were encouraged to question, take risks and try new things. The survey also found
that employees believed that they learned most effectively from workplace learning
opportunities, with coaching and mentoring considered highly effective ways of helping
individuals to learn. This latter aspect resonates with Gould and Baldwin's (2004) study of
social work and learning organisations, with the need for practitioners to be given time to
learn at work. They describe the difficulties practitioners found in persuading their organi-
sations to grant space for reflective activities, and without these opportunities there was
little chance of developing strategies for effective practice.

Comment

We can see in the above paragraph and research summary that the culture of an organisation is a significant factor in its effectiveness. Where practices need improvement it can sometimes be difficult to introduce change due to the strength of established beliefs (Scragg, 2010). Organisational cultures that have evolved over time about how a service is managed and delivered can be so much part of everyday practice that they go unquestioned. These beliefs and assumptions about a service can be unspoken and taken for granted – 'the way we do things around here'. Where organisations fail to make needed improvements, the power of a culture can be a major factor in resistance to change. Attempting to change a service often means challenging existing beliefs and assumptions about a service (Scragg, 2011). This can require a fundamental rethink about what constitutes good practice in order to promote a new cultural paradigm (Johnson and Scholes, 2008).

Opportunities for using reflective practice

Reflective learning takes place through an understanding of professional knowledge developed in practice and the systematic analysis of that experience (Gould, 1996). Using this approach, reflective practice involves drawing selectively and appropriately on our professional knowledge base, integrating theory with practice, rather than relying on theory to provide ready-made answers. In this way we learn from experience by reflecting on it and being open to new ideas.

Front-line managers and their staff have a range of opportunities available to them where reflection-on-practice can take place. The following examples are provided to give you some ideas about the possibilities open to you and your manager.

Supervision

Supervision provides a unique opportunity for supporting staff and providing a context for the development of reflective practice. Supervision most usefully needs to address four key functions (Morrison, 1993):

- responsibility for managing the supervisee's work;

- providing emotional and practical support;

- helping the supervisee's professional development;

- acting as a channel of communication between front-line staff and middle and senior management.

It is through the process of reflection in supervision sessions that professional learning can take place, both in analysing the explanations and the evidence on which assessments and interventions were based and identifying where there are developmental needs in relation to practice. This requires the supervisor and supervisee to separate out what went well and what hindered practice interventions, so that they can first articulate for themselves and then communicate to clients what has underpinned their assessments and their choice of interventions, and thereby use supervision to provide accountability to people using the service as well as governance of the service (Cunningham, 2004).

Critically appraising practice in this way should not be seen as a personal attack on the supervisee's practice, but a valuable external perspective that can offer new insights and angles on a problem. This process will be more effective where the organisational culture is non-defensive and values learning, and where practitioners feel comfortable when the supervisor challenges their judgements and assumptions (Munro, 2011).

Practitioners benefit from the process of knowledge that can be learnt from high-quality supervision. This is where managers focus on the developmental aspects of supervision, although this can often be neglected under the pressure of work, with time and opportunity to share and reflect on practice – for example, time for debate and development of critical thinking skills – submerged by the focus on micro-details of individual cases (Sawdon and Sawdon, 1995). The pressure on front-line managers to monitor the performance of staff and focus on the need to meet quantifiable outcomes risks undermining the practitioners' ability to think creatively, which challenges the rational-technical approach that has stifled social work practice (Munro, 2011).

A more reflective approach where there is time to mull over experience and learn from it avoids what Thompson (2000) describes as a routinised response to practice where practitioners come to rely on routines that are applied in complex situations, often inappropriately, stemming from (among other things) the use of untested assumptions, reliance on stereotypes and missed opportunities for learning and professional development. It is the front-line manager's responsibility to ensure that a team or organisational culture does not encourage a routinised approach in spite of organisational pressures towards conformity. In her research, Ruch (2005) has challenged bureaucratic responses to the complexity, risk and uncertainty in social work, and has argued for a more creative and thoughtful approach to practice, recognising diverse sources of knowledge that are embedded in practice as well as theoretical perspectives.

ACTIVITY 9.2

Reflect on your experience of supervision. How far did the session address the main functions of supervision?

If the session did not meet your needs, can you identify what aspect of supervision was unsuccessful?

- *Was it to do with location?*
- *Was it to do with structure?*
- *Was it to do with the content?*
- *Was it to do with the process?*
- *Was it related to your manager's contribution?*
- *Was it related to your own contribution?*
- *What could your manager do to ensure that the next session is more successful?*
- *What could you do to ensure that your next session is more successful?*

Comment

This activity should have helped you judge the effectiveness of your supervision sessions and whether they are meeting your needs. If they are not, it could be concerned with a lack of clarity about the expectation that both you and your supervisor have about supervision and its purpose. A contract that sets out the purpose, processes, practical arrangements and expectations of supervision can help create a more effective supervisory relationship in the future.

Consultation

A second area that provides an opportunity for reflection is consultation. This is a problem-solving process where you can use your manager as a consultant. The difference between consultation and supervision is that it can be a one-off event for which you (as consultee) set the agenda, while your manager's role (as consultant) is to facilitate your working through a specific issue that concerns you. You are drawing on the experience and expertise of another person who can offer you the help you need. You can, of course, use other people from your team, or in the wider service if you feel they have the particular expertise to help you.

Using Schein's (1987) approach to consultation, it is a process where your manager, acting in the role of consultant, works collaboratively with you in a manner that enables you to develop your own assessment of the issue and use your skills to act. This process is as follows:

- Stage one: active listening on the part of the manager as they encourage you to describe the issue that concerns you, and try to understand the issues from your perspective.

- Stage two: diagnostic intervention, which focuses on helping you to think about what is going on in the situation through reflection on previous actions or interventions.

- Stage three: action alternatives, when the focus shifts to what you want to consider in terms of action and you begin to describe action that will follow the consultation.

Ideally your manager will ask you questions that stimulate you to form your own ideas as to why events have occurred and what might be done. This also takes the pressure off the manager of having to be the expert and provide solutions, and in turn helps you to come to a judgement about the issue and to learn about the process of problem-solving. In this way consultation provides a valuable opportunity to reflect on a practice situation and through a problem-solving process build your confidence to act in the future, and also to experience using the expertise of your manager in a non-managerial relationship.

CASE STUDY

Paul has been asked to take responsibility for working with a client where a succession of workers have tried a range of interventions, without success. He is concerned that his intervention will lead to similar frustrations and has asked his manager Sarah if she will help him to work through some of the issues and discuss various approaches to work with the client. She agrees to meet with him and discuss his concerns. Her approach is not to suggest how he approaches the client, but to explore the issues, probe and test his assumptions and support him to make his own decisions about the options he could consider when he meets the client for the first time. In this way she hopes to help Paul become more confident in his practice, and also to model an approach to problem-solving where her team members do not become dependent on her for answers to problems, but develop confidence in their own problem-solving abilities.

To work effectively in a consultative relationship it is important that you take responsibility for how you want to work with your manager (or another member of the team) in a consultative role, including:

- openly sharing your concerns about the issue and why you need help in thinking through your approach;

- accepting constructive feedback from your manager;

- participating in problem-solving and not expecting to be told what to do;

- reflecting on the issues and exploring options open to you;

- taking responsibility for implementing the action you have decided on.

Reviewing and evaluating interventions

A further opportunity to review practice and in turn reflect on the effectiveness of interventions can be undertaken by evaluating practice. Although supervisory sessions and consultation provide opportunities for reflection, other contexts are also important to develop these skills. Review and evaluation are parts of the five stages of systematic practice: assessment, intervention, review, termination and evaluation (Thompson, 2000).

Reviewing practice enables the practitioner and their manager to explore current approaches and whether adjustments need to be made in the plan, or radically different tactics need to be used. A client's situation can change over time and assessment may need to change too as an initial assessment may have been based on partial information. It is important, then, that practice is reviewed periodically so that adjustments can be made to the intervention plan. A consequence of not reviewing practice regularly is that time, effort and energy can be wasted because the intervention is misdirected. The review gives you an opportunity to amend or confirm your plan of intervention.

Once an intervention is completed there is the opportunity to evaluate what worked and what was less successful, and what can be learned from the process. This process should take you back to the initial assessment and your original objectives and how far you were able to meet these and what was not achieved, given the time, resources and priorities (Thompson, 2000).

Evaluation of interventions is also important, not only in terms of specific interventions but also in relation to the organisation, which needs to review the effectiveness of the services it provides where resources are limited. A key part of evaluation is the need for practitioners to understand that it can enhance the effectiveness, accountability and transparency of practice. From a wider perspective it is increasingly expected by those who fund services and those who use them, so that together evaluating interventions and outcomes enables practitioners to be more effective and efficient (Alston and Bowles, 2003).

Evaluation is also an important element in practitioners developing a research-mindedness approach to their practice, and countering the risks when so much practice *inevitably happens on the hoof without the opportunity for critical evaluation* (Gould and Baldwin, 2004, p46). Evaluating your practice periodically has the potential to help you develop more effective interventions by adopting a research approach to your practice with the potential to improve it and ensure that you remain conscious of the need for continual improvement. Review and evaluation has a further potentially important role in providing the social work profession with the evidence to demonstrate its effectiveness and respond to attacks that stem from politically driven agendas which undermine the confidence and morale of practitioners.

RESEARCH SUMMARY

The Management of Practice Expertise Project undertaken by the former National Institute for Social Work had as one of its aims to identify which kind of approaches to management enabled staff to develop and sustain their practice expertise. This was conducted through a survey of supervision arrangements and policies in social services departments, a study of a group of practice sites and conferences, and workshops that brought together managers and practitioners to explore relationships between management, supervision and practice development. In a discussion paper published as part of the research, it found that front-line managers were vital to the practice and service delivery of an organisation and that they were the keystones between senior management and front-line staff, their teams and other teams, and between the agency and other services and individuals. The key role of the front-line manager was concerned with holding together the different worlds and avoiding the damaging fragmentation if these different worlds did not maintain relationships with each other. Further important roles were the deployment of resources and ensuring that standards in practices were set and maintained, that staff were supported when engaging in complex and demanding practice, and that they were continually developed in knowledge-based practice. This is particularly achieved where the managers model practice and their work is visible, for example in residential settings and where they act as consultants to team members, playing the role of crucial opinion leaders (Rosen, 2000).

Conclusion

Developing an effective working relationship with your manager is a crucial part of your development as a social worker. How you build this relationship will be important in defining how far you move beyond a comfortable openness in your dialogue to a position where you can explore more of your biases and interpretations and articulate your reasons for particular approaches to intervention that can lead to real change in your practice. Much of the success of this relationship will also depend on your manager and how far they have developed their own skills in reflecting on their practice and how far they are able to move beyond defensive routines that have become such a powerful part of the prevailing ethos in many organisations and thus be willing to explore the complex world of social work practice.

CHAPTER SUMMARY

The role of front-line managers has changed significantly, from the traditional focus on supporting practice to one that more closely resembles that of the general manager, with responsibilities for the efficient management of resources, the effective performance of staff and the achievement of the strategic goals of the organisation, using their positional power to influence change. Front-line managers are increasingly balancing the demands of the organisation with the need to ensure the maintenance and support of practice as a result of the managerialist ethos in social care organisations. You can significantly influence your relationship with your line manager through the adoption of a proactive and positive approach to managing this important relationship. Working with your manager to develop a mutually satisfactory working relationship can benefit you both, and in turn service users and the wider organisation, as your practice improves and develops. Front-line managers have a wide range of methods available to them to support your development, through supervision, consultation and evaluation of your practice. Each has the potential to use reflection as

(Continued)

a means of widening your understanding of practice. Knowing how to take advantage of the different techniques available can help you decide how your manager can best support you. Working with your manager to explore the complexities of practice means a degree of openness and willingness to challenge assumptions that can be uncomfortable but has the potential to open your practice to deeper examination.

FURTHER READING

Scragg, T (2009) *Managing at the front line: A handbook for managers in social care*, 2nd edition. Brighton: OLM-Pavilion.

This book provides a wide-ranging exploration of the work of the front-line manager combining theoretical perspectives with the views of managers and staff in social care services.

Hafford-Letchfield, T (2009) *Management and organisations in social work*, 2nd edition. London: Sage.

Explores a wide range of key issues in the management of social work organisations, including such issues as leadership, culture and performance.

Statham, D (2004) (ed.) *Managing front line practice in social care*. London: Jessica Kingsley.

This book proves a valuable insight into how managers can support practitioners, emphasising knowledge-based practice and professional development.

REFERENCES

Alston, M and Bowles, W (2003) *Research for social workers: An introduction to methods*, 2nd edition. London: Routledge.

Chartered Institute of Personnel and Development (2004) *Training and development: Survey report.* Available at: www.cipd.co.uk (accessed 30 March 2013).

Cunningham, G (2004) Supervision and governance. In D Statham (ed.), *Managing front line practice in social care.* London: Jessica Kingsley.

Darvill, G (1997) *The management of work-based learning: A guide for managers of social care and social work on raising standards of practice.* London: The Stationery Office.

Eraut, M (2001) Learning challenges for knowledge-based organisations. In J Stevens (ed.), *Workplace learning in Europe.* London: Chartered Institute of Personnel and Development.

Gould, N (1996) Introduction: Social work education and the 'crisis of the professions'. In N Gould and I Taylor (eds), *Reflective learning for social work.* Aldershot: Arena.

Gould, N and Baldwin, M (2004) *Social work, critical reflection and the learning organization.* Aldershot: Ashgate.

Henderson, J and Seden, J (2003) What do we want from social care managers? Aspirations and realities. In J Reynolds, I Henderson, J Seden, J Charlesworth and A Bullman (eds), *The managing care reader.* London: Routledge and the Open University.

Johnson, K and Scholes, P. (2008) *Exploring corporate strategy*, 8th edition. Harlow: Pearson Education.

Kearney, P (2004) First line managers, the mediator of standards and quality of practice. In D Statham (ed.), *Managing front line practice in social care.* London: Jessica Kingsley.

Morrison, T (1993) *Staff supervision in social care: An action learning approach.* Brighton: Pavilion.

Munro, E. (2011) *The Munro Report: Final Report – a child-centred system.* London: Department of Education.

Rosen, G (ed.) (2000) *Integrity, the organisation and the first-line manager: Discussion papers.* London: National Institute for Social Work.

Ruch, G (2005) Relationship-based practice and reflective practice: holistic approaches to contemporary child care social work. *Child and Family Social Work*, 10(2): 111–23.

Sawdon, C and Sawdon, D (1995) The supervision partnership: a whole greater than the sum of its parts. In J Pritchard (ed.), *Good practice in supervision.* London: Jessica Kingsley.

Schein, E H (1987) *Process consultation, volume 11: Lessons for managers and consultants.* Reading, MA: Addison-Wesley.

Scragg, T (2009) *Managing at the front line: A handbook for managers in social care*, 2nd edition. Brighton: OLM-Pavilion.

Scragg, T (2010) *Managing change in health and social care services.* Brighton: Pavilion.

Scragg, T (2011) Organisational cultures and the management of change. In T Scragg and A Mantell (eds), *Safeguarding adults in social work*, 2nd edition. London: Sage.

Smith, R (2010) *Social work, risk, power.* Available at: www.socresonline.org.uk (accessed 15 October 2015).

Thompson, N (2000) *Understanding social work: Preparing for practice.* Basingstoke: Macmillan.

Thompson, S and Thompson, N (2008) *The critically reflective practitioner.* Basingstoke: Palgrave Macmillan.

Chapter 10

Reflective practice for collaborative working

Janet McCray

Introduction

Collaborative working with a range of partners is part of daily professional practice. Recent legislative changes, for example the Health and Social Care Act (Safety and Quality) (DOH, 2015), and a person-centred system of care (DOH, 2012, p11), underpin all aspects of intervention. The transformation of services has increased the scope, type and range of partnerships. For social workers, much of this collaborative practice has taken place within an interprofessional context; however, the range of professional networks and the nature of partnerships for collaboration are shifting, particularly in partnership with third sector partners, and require new ways of working. At the same time the constant and familiar challenges presented by agency boundaries and limited resources remain, and the pace of change is unprecedented. Emerging and new partnerships place further demands on the professional leadership role necessary to offer good models of service delivery, one consequence being an increased emphasis on the leadership and managerial skills of social care practice. For social workers and other professionals this may result in the need to re-evaluate their leadership strategies and managerial strengths in order to work more effectively. This chapter explores the use of reflection to assist in effective leadership strategies supported through the application of a practice learning tool.

ACTIVITY **10.1**

Questions to ask yourself at the beginning of this chapter:

- *What methods do I use currently to reflect on my collaborative working leadership role?*
- *Are they useful in evaluating my practice?*
- *Do I share them openly with others in a formal or informal setting?*
- *How successful are they for me?*

What is collaborative working?

A number of terms are used in the literature to define collaborative working and many are used interchangeably to describe it. A simple definition is: a respect for other professionals and service users and their skills and from this starting point, an agreed sharing of authority, responsibility and resources for specific outcomes or actions, gained through co-operation and consensus.

Early definitions of collaboration have included this from Kanter (1994, p96):

> *a process that enables independent individuals and organisations to combine their human and material resources so they can accomplish objectives they are unable to bring about alone*

while Gray (1989, p5) describes collaboration as:

> *a process through which parties who see different aspects of a problem can explore constructively their differences and search for solutions that go beyond their differences and search for solutions that go beyond their own limited vision of what is possible.*

Ansari and Phillips describe collaboration as *an advanced shared vision* (2001, p119). From a human service delivery perspective, Percy Smith observes: *agencies working together in a wide variety of different ways to pursue a common goal whilst also pursuing organisational goals* (2005, p24).

Specifically in social work and social work education, Taylor et al. (2006, p15), in their research review of partnership working, note:

> there are a plethora of terms to be grappled with, including participation and partnership, involvement and collaboration as well as interprofessional, interdisciplinary, multiprofessional, shared or joint practice to name but a few.

They continue by noting that only a minority explicitly define partnership working, nor do the potential tensions it creates receive much coverage in the social work literature (Taylor et al., 2006, p15). D'Amour et al. (2005) have explored the core concepts of collaboration in the literature, one of which includes aspects of sharing, such as having a collegiate relationship, shared responsibilities, shared decision-making and shared data.

Often collaborative working forms an element of multi-professional and multi-agency teamwork, an approach reflected in the social work literature (Taylor et al., 2006, p19). For the purpose of this chapter this represents a useful starting point and encompasses the breadth of the activities and partnerships that may be involved.

ACTIVITY 10.2

- *What does collaborative working involve?*
- *Spend a few minutes listing the knowledge and skills required.*

Comment

You may have included:

- making time to get to know other professionals and their roles and how they may be evolving in new contexts;
- thinking about language and terms used and their relevance and meaning to other professionals or workers;
- exploring your own prejudices about other professional groups and their models of practice;
- reflecting on values and not making assumptions about shared beliefs or views;
- being clear about resources and their impact on collaboration;
- being confident about your professional practice and ability in the collaborative working role;

- being credible – delivering as promised to action plans and keeping others involved informed of progress;

- gaining consensus on leadership and accountability in a specific practice situation.

Leadership in collaborative working

Designing, developing and evaluating leadership styles, types and models has been a major task of researchers and practitioners in all sectors of service delivery. As the literature demonstrates, the popularity of leadership styles or types tends to reflect a particular political or socio-economic view. In her introduction to leadership in the twenty-first century, Jasper (2005, p3) cites Avery (2004) who observes that the challenge for leadership is to *operate under rapidly mutating circumstances, which require a rethink of paradigms of leadership both in theory and practice* (p7).

Traditionally, transactional leadership underpinned by social exchange theory has been applied most frequently based on a hierarchical model of leadership in public sector management. In this model leaders and managers set goals and objectives while workers are rewarded or penalised based on their progress towards achieving them. However, new models of service delivery with an emphasis on collaboration may require a broader range of relationships and partnerships, as a more complex set of boundaries and accountabilities may make reliance solely on a transactional model less feasible and effective. The involvement of service user and carers requires different leadership strategies, while serious case reviews in adult and child protection have made the need for compassionate leadership a shared vision for health and social care organisations (West et al., 2015). Emphasis is on all leaders within organisations and teams being aligned on delivering services, which sets high-quality care as the priority to avoid the breakdown of collaborative care and support (Bezrukova et al., 2012).

The transformational leadership style (Burns, 1978) remains important. Munir et al. (2012) cite the positive effects of a transformational leadership role on service user outcomes, safety, and service user and staff satisfaction. Bate (1994) describes one of the responsibilities of a leader as being that of *creating the conditions to release potential energy* (p244), thus describing the facilitation role that is a key characteristic of transformational leadership. In this model, leaders share goals with workers and explore together methods and strategies for achieving them. Thus all work together to gain rewards. Bass (1990) advocates transformational skills, especially that of 'intellectual stimulation', to facilitate collaborative team-working. A further critical element of transformational leadership is responsiveness to change while constantly developing new networks and practising effectively (Hackett and Spurgeon, 1998, p171). Equally, emotional resilience is necessary for leaders (McCray and Palmer, 2014). Anderson and West (1998, p235) offer a taxonomy of transforming practices which include communication, counselling and consultation, underpinned by self-awareness and self-management.

Leadership in practice

Think about your own role in practice.

- *What models of leadership do you use?*
- *In what sort of situations?*
- *Are they effective for collaborative working?*

Examples of leadership in practice

Transactional leadership

The problem: On reviewing a number of individual service user profiles held as a caseload by a staff member you note several who have not had assessments or visits for some time.

The response: You are not aware of a strong reason for this from the worker's perspective. You, as the manager, first check that this is the case and then decide on a date for rectifying this, and inform the staff member of your decision.

Transformational leadership

The problem: At a team meeting, a team member notes that changes to the configuration of the local primary care trust mean that some nursing professionals will be moving base and taking on new roles. As a leader you think this may be significant for future working and alliances, particularly around supporting children with disability.

The response: You ask the group what the issues might be and what new strategies might be required to ensure continued collaboration. Following discussion, a plan is drawn up by the team to explore the issues and a leader (not yourself) is identified and agreed by the team to take this forward.

Collaborative working

Both models may be effective in collaboration, especially when results or outputs are viewed by other professionals or workers as evidence of commitment and credibility. For example, a professional who does not regularly review their caseload will not be viewed positively by others; hence it may be appropriate to use a hierarchical leadership model here. Equally, when new situations happen and changes in working patterns occur, a different approach and response to problem-solving with shared leadership may be more effective.

Using reflection to assist in the effective leadership of collaborative working

Earlier in the chapter we revisited some of the components of reflection and how they can assist in practice. Brief explorations of collaborative working and leadership have been presented and you have had the opportunity to reflect on your collaborative leadership role and style. It is now time to think more about enhancing collaboration through reflection.

The framework in Figure 10.1 has been developed to act as a guide, model or toolkit for practice. At its simplest it acts as an express checklist to focus thinking or action before, during or after a collaborative working intervention. However, it may also be used as a tool for deeper reflection on practice, helping to support exploration of a number of components of collaborative working from a specific starting point.

About the framework

The components in the framework were originally developed through research with nurses and social workers in the field of learning disability (McCray, 2003). Through exploring practice activity around multi-professional working, key concepts or components of good practice were developed. These components were placed in order drawing on practitioners' experience and the research evidence available. For example, the practitioners in the original study had suggested that it was no use working to empower service users without knowledge of the person themselves and the

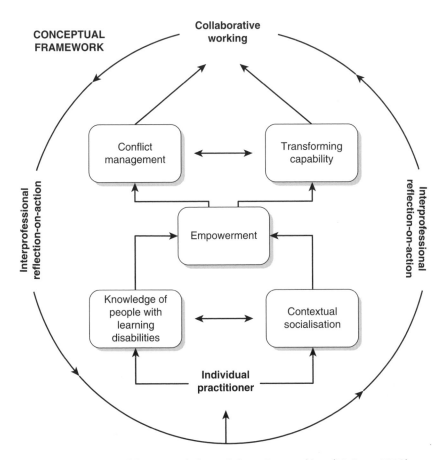

Figure 10.1 *A conceptual framework for collaborative working (McCray, 2003)*

context in which the empowerment was needed. If we look at the literature on collaboration and interagency working, a key factor in leading teams is credibility (Hudson, 1999, p15). If time is not taken to gain knowledge and understanding of a situation, then when asked to support or intervene the contribution may not be credible. Thus a leader would not gain support for a different response from the other professionals involved. Further action to enable service users to make changes for themselves would not be seen as credible.

Only through attention to the person (knowledge of the person – the first component) and the context (contextual socialisation – the second component) is empowerment (the third component of the framework) of the practitioner or service users and carers or other staff likely. The key to this attention is reflection-on-action (interprofessional reflection-on-action – the sixth component) which Mantell describes in Chapter 5 as an outcome-driven activity or review. In this model this process is undertaken at each stage of the collaborative working action with a focus on what the individual may have done differently (if anything) at each point through to what the individual might need to change for future intervention or strategies.

Participants in the original study questioned the use of power in interprofessional collaboration. They observed that without being and feeling empowered themselves, they were unable to empower others or feel comfortable sharing power with service users and carers. They suggested that transforming leaders work towards a basis for practice underpinned by mutual, value-focused agreement in order to create positive social change. Only through addressing and recognising power issues (Component 3, Empowerment) can the practitioner begin to create and plan for real change (Component 4, Transforming capability) and design and or apply new methods for recognising and responding to any conflict created (Component 5, Conflict management). Once again, attention is paid to the effectiveness of these strategies using reflection-on-action.

Using the framework

CASE STUDY

You are the lead social worker supporting Sophia, aged 15, and her family. Sophia is a young person with physical and learning disabilities who lives at home in a supportive and close-knit family. Sophia has had good educational and children's service health care support through her life, but as she draws near to school-leaving age and moves towards adult services, she and her family have been expressing concerns about the future, and the opportunities for continued health care support and potential employment opportunities. At a recent review meeting Sophia and her family voiced these concerns and the lack of future plans in place for her transition to more adult-focused services. Major worries were gaps in terms of links with adult health services for monitoring and treatment of her physical disability, and access to learning disability agencies' support. Following this meeting you contacted your professional colleagues in health about Sophia's future needs and provision before a further meeting with Sophia and her family.

Preparation for collaboration

As you prepare for the meeting with health colleagues, you use the Reflective Framework to help you. Your starting point is your current knowledge of Sophia and her family (Component 1). You ask yourself a number of questions related to them:

- *Have you adequate knowledge about their views on needs for the future?*

- *Is this knowledge recent or does it require reviewing? Are Sophia and her family happy for you to act on their behalf?*

- *Have you enough knowledge to act with credibility?*

Given exploration of the knowledge element, you reflect on the context (Component 2) in which multi-professional collaboration is taking place. You ask yourself a number of questions, which might include the following.

- *What is the impact of Sophia's transition into adult services on the family?*

- *Are any social or economic factors involved?*

- *Will more or a different form of support be required if Sophia leaves full-time education?*

- *Am I familiar with acute health care service processes or do I have the appropriate multi-professional links to gain access to those services?*

- *Would there be new resource issues to work through as Sophia has a number of health care needs?*

- *What is the current situation like for others in transition using these local health care services?*

Comment

In exploring these questions you might reflect also on your preparation for leadership in this context:

- What sort of links do you have with other professionals in adult services in health care?

- How effective have they been?

- What factors have influenced their effectiveness, for example political, economic or other?

- Do these experiences impact on planning your leadership strategy for this current multi-professional collaboration?

At this point the next component of the reflective model is empowerment (Component 3), focusing upon the use and place of power in this context.

Think about your responses to the critical reflection commentary so far. What sort of questions might you explore in relation to the empowerment component (Component 3)?

Comment

You may have included:

- How much involvement has Sophia had in planning her transition to adult services so far?

- What role have her family played?

- What other professionals are involved in the transition process and what role do they play?

- To what extent are resources an issue in relation to empowerment and choice?

- What is my role and where can my power be used most effectively?

As you progress through the model you should be building a picture of your role and leadership strengths and needs in this situation. It may be that this is all very positive and you are affirming your multi-professional leadership skills and knowledge. Alternatively, there may be areas of development required that the reflective activity is highlighting. For example, your reflection might also be bringing out the conflict that could be present as debates with other professionals get under way. You may need to ask yourself a number of questions about conflict management (Component 5).

You may need to explore the following questions.

- How safe do you feel in a conflict management situation?

- What is the nature of the conflict being presented?

- Where can the conflict be addressed – in the team setting, or in some other arena?

- What conflict management models could be used?

- Can the conflict be ignored?

- What are the consequences of ignoring the source of conflict?

- As leader of the team, are you the appropriate person to deal with the conflict?

- What would be the impact of conflict on collaborative working relationships?

Having worked through potential responses to any conflict and its management and decided on a solution, only then are you in a position to create change (Component 4, Transforming capability).

At this point an action plan can be made and you might reflect on the following.

- How supportive will the team be of your approach and outline plan for Sophia?

- What information around resources needs to be highlighted?

- What other new skills, networks and or information do I need?

- Can a timeframe be put in place?

- Are there any team members who may choose not to collaborate?

- How close is the likely outcome of the collaborative process to Sophia's family's wishes?

- What form of leadership is likely to work to manage the change process?

Finally, having worked through all the components of the framework, you can return to its starting point and reflect on the effectiveness of your collaborative working leadership and what you have learned.

ACTIVITY **10.6**

Using the framework for your practice

Having seen an example of the framework's use with the case study above, you should now try it out using an example from your own collaborative working caseload. Before you begin this, remind yourself of your responses to the initial questions about your collaborative working leadership style at the beginning of the chapter.

- *What methods do I use currently to reflect on my collaborative working leadership role?*

- *Are they useful in evaluating my practice?*

- *Do I share them openly with others in a formal or informal setting?*

- *How successful are they for me?*

Comment

After you have worked through your own case, you might also wish to reflect on your initial responses to the questions about your leadership style.

- Are your current methods effective and successful?

- Do you need to develop new approaches or tools to support you in practice?

- Can the framework add to your current methods of reflection and evaluation?

- Does the framework add a further means of support for reflection?

- If the framework is not useful to you, what other tool might be?

- What have you learned about your collaborative working style from this process?

- Have you identified areas requiring additional professional development?

CHAPTER SUMMARY

This chapter has introduced collaborative working leadership. It has presented a practical tool to aid reflection on collaborative working leadership using a series of exercises and a case study. Throughout, a number of activities and reflective cues have placed emphasis on your own practice and thinking as a social work practitioner. By reading the chapter you may have gained new insights into your collaborative working role and leadership style and highlighted areas for CPD. Alternatively, you may have affirmed your current collaborative working style and reflective activity.

Whichever is the case, what remains certain is that there will be an increasing need for social workers to be equipped with collaborative working leadership skills. Further reflection on the attributes required and your individual readiness for the role will both support and enhance your future professional development.

FURTHER READING

Barrett, GS, Ellman, D and Thomas, J (2005) *Interprofessional working for health and social care.* Basingstoke: Palgrave Macmillan.

This book provides the case for interprofessional working and looks at the impact on a range of professional groups and their practice.

Mullins, LJ (2009) *Essentials of management and organizational behavior.* London: Prentice Hall.

A useful management textbook with examples from health and social care looking at management and leadership in organisations and teams.

Quinney, A (2006) *Collaborative social work practice.* Exeter: Learning Matters.

This book offers you more detailed information about collaboration in social work practice

REFERENCES

Anderson, NR and West, MA (1998) Measuring the climate for work group innovation: development and validation of the team climate inventory. *Journal of Organisational Behaviour,* 19: 235–38.

Ansari, W and Phillips, CJ (2001) Partnerships, community participation and intersectoral collaboration in South Africa. *Journal of Interprofessional Care,* 15(2): 119–32.

Avery, GC (2004) *Understanding leadership.* London: Sage.

Bass, B (1990) From transactional to transformational leadership: learning to share the vision. *Organizational Dynamics,* 18(3): 19–31.

Bate, P (1994) *Strategies for cultural change.* Oxford: Butterworth-Heinemann.

Bezrukova, K, Thatcher, SMB, Jehn, KA and Spell, CS (2012) The effects of alignment examining group faultlines, organizational cultures and performance. *Journal of Applied Psychology,* 97(1): 77–92.

Burns, JM (1978) *Leadership.* New York: Harper and Row.

D'Amour, D, Ferradai-Vidella, M, San Martin Rodriguez, L and Beaulieu, MD (2005) The conceptual basis for interprofessional collaboration: core concepts and theoretical frameworks. *Journal of Interprofessional Care,* 1: 116–31.

Department of Health (2012) *Caring for our future: Reforming our care and support.* London: HMSO.

Department of Health (2015) The Health and Social Care (Safety and Quality) Act. London: HMSO.

Gray, B (1989) *Collaborating: Finding common ground for multiparty problems*. San Francisco: Jossey-Bass.

Hackett, M and Spurgeon, P (1998) Developing our leaders in the future. *Health Manpower Management*, 24(5): 170–77.

Hudson, B (1999) Primary health care and social care: working across professional boundaries. *Managing Community Care*, 7(1): 15–22.

Jasper, M (2005) The challenges of healthcare leadership in Britain today. In M Jasper and M Jumaa (eds), *Effective healthcare leadership*. Oxford: Blackwell.

Kanter, RM (1994) Collaborative advantage: the art of alliances. *Harvard Business Review*, July–August: 96–108.

McCray, J (2003) Leading interprofessional practice: a conceptual framework to support practitioners in the field of learning disability. *Journal of Nursing Management*, 11: 387–95.

McCray, J and Palmer, A (2014) Commissioning personalised care in the English adult social care sector: using action research as a framework to support leadership development. *Social Care and Neurodisability*, 5(1): 3–15.

Munir, F, Nielson, K, Garde, H, Albertson, K and Carneiro, G (2012) Mediating the effects of work life conflict between transformational leadership and health care workers job satisfaction and psychological well being. *Journal of Nursing Management*, 20(4): 512.

Percy Smith, J (2005) *What works in strategic partnerships for children*. Essex: Barnados.

Taylor, I, Sharland, E, Sebba, J, Leviche, P, Keep, E and Orr, D (2006) *The learning, teaching and assessment of partnership work in social work education*. Bristol: Policy Press.

West, M, Armit, K, Loewenthal, L, Eckert, R, West, T and Lee, A (2015) *Leadership and leadership development in health care*. London: King's Fund.

Conclusion

This book has covered a range of topics from the perspective of reflective practice. It has introduced you to the concepts that have informed our understanding of reflective practice, the way knowledge is potentially used by professionals and what you need to consider if you are to become an effective practitioner. By understanding how you can become a more skilled reflective practitioner we hope it will help you narrow the gap between the theory and practice of social work and generate practice-based knowledge that can guide your actions.

Social work deals with people who need practitioners to be responsive and reflective instead of simply carrying out everyday practice in a routine or ritualistic manner. Reflection on practice can help you guard against the risks of 'working on autopilot' in which you follow the same pattern of practice that governs and directs your action. It provides the opportunity to focus on your practice and confront, understand and work towards resolving the contradictions that are inherent in much social work practice.

In the first part of this book (Chapters 1 and 2) we provided you with some of the key concepts that have informed the development of reflective practice and a range of processes that you can adopt to develop your own skills in reflection on and about your practice, with examples of some of the methods that can be used when you first engage in reflection on your practice and to which you can return throughout your social work career. In these chapters we cautioned you about the risks associated with technical and rational assumptions about practice, in situations that are often messy and uncertain, where the value of reflection on and about your practice can help you understand, learn and discover new approaches that reconcile some of the contradictions within social work practice.

The second part focused on a range of techniques and issues that can be illuminated and enhanced by using techniques of reflection. First, we looked at understanding the role of your emotions (Chapter 3) and how emotional intelligence can help you explore more fully your responses to practice issues. This was followed (Chapter 4) by an example of how you can use techniques adapted from cognitive behaviour therapy to examine your own thought patterns and develop more confidence at a personal and practice level. Drawing on recent research (Chapter 5), we examined work with carers that raises important questions about the role of service users and carers in the social work relationship and alerts you to some of the complex issues involved when you are working in these situations. We then considered (Chapter 6) an area that is important to all social workers, that of working with service users who are hostile and aggressive. Our intention was to demonstrate how you can use reflection to more fully understand risk and minimise professional dangerousness in your practice. We then examined the role of gender in social work (Chapter 7) and some of the key issues that are important to understand as you explore gender both in the student setting and in practice situations. The influence of gender in terms of personal identity and also the expectations of others was discussed, as well as the importance of understanding how it may impact on you in practice situations. Finally in this section (Chapter 8), we examined reflective practice from the standpoint of the practice placement. This chapter is intended to help you understand how you can use a variety of different approaches when reflecting on practice and gain more from your placement in partnership with your practice educator.

The third and final part focused on management and how reflective practice can be promoted and maintained through a range of management and organisational processes. We first explored the world of the front-line manager (Chapter 9) and their crucial role in maintaining the balance between the demands of practice and the demands of the wider organisation, with suggestions of ways you can manage your relationship with your manager, and some of the techniques that you can use to reflect on and about practice with your manager. Finally, we acknowledged in Chapter 10 that social work increasingly takes place in an interprofessional context, and how leadership, at all levels, is essential to effective social work and service delivery. We aim in these two chapters to provide you with a deeper understanding of the world of management and the interprofessional context which you will begin to experience as a student on placement and will engage with more fully as your career develops.

We hope that you have found this book helpful in providing an insight into how you can develop your practice using concepts and techniques of reflection, and stimulating you to test out approaches to reflection that provide an opportunity to explore your experiences with your practice educator. We also hope that once you are qualified you will retain a commitment to reflective practice as part of your CPD, making time to engage in reflection, and be willing to challenge current practice where it fails to provide satisfactory answers, recognising that there is no end point to learning for the effective social work practitioner.

Appendix 1

Professional Capabilities Framework

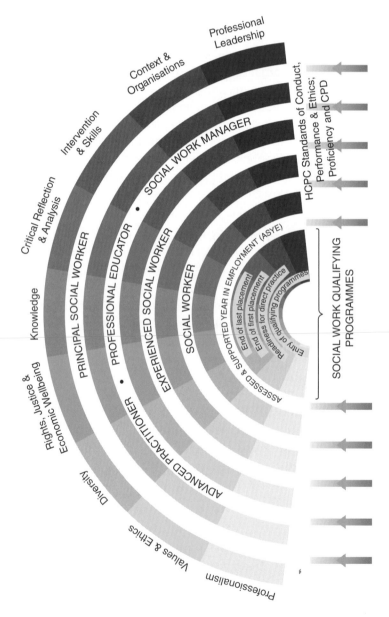

Professional Capabilities Framework diagram reproduced with permission of The College of Social Work.

Appendix 2
Subject benchmark for social work

3 Nature and extent of social work

3.1 This subject benchmark statement covers social work as an applied academic subject at honours level. It sets out expectations concerning:

- the subject knowledge, understanding and skills of an honours graduate in social work;

- the teaching, learning and assessment methods employed in their education;

- the standards expected of them at the point of graduation.

3.2 Legislation establishing regulatory bodies in social work and introducing statutory registration of social workers was passed across the UK from 2000 onwards. These acts also recognise the terms 'social work' and/or 'social worker' as protected titles. Anyone using the title 'social worker' is required to be registered with the relevant care council.

4 Defining principles

4.6 Social work is a moral activity that requires practitioners to recognise the dignity of the individual, but also to make and implement difficult decisions (including restriction of liberty) in human situations that involve the potential for benefit or harm. Honours degree programmes in social work therefore involve the study, application of, and critical reflection upon, ethical principles and dilemmas. As reflected by the four care councils' codes of practice, this involves showing respect for persons, honouring the diverse and distinctive organisations and communities that make up contemporary society, promoting social justice and combating processes that lead to discrimination, marginalisation and social exclusion. This means that honours undergraduates must learn to:

- recognise and work with the powerful links between intrapersonal and interpersonal factors and the wider social, legal, economic, political and cultural context of people's lives;

- understand the impact of injustice, social inequalities and oppressive social relations;

- challenge constructively individual, institutional and structural discrimination;

- practise in ways that maximise safety and effectiveness in situations of uncertainty and incomplete information;

- help people to gain, regain or maintain control of their own affairs, insofar as this is compatible with their own or others' safety, wellbeing and rights;

- work in partnership with service users and carers and other professionals to foster dignity, choice and independence, and effect change.

4.7 The expectation that social workers will be able to act effectively in such complex circumstances requires that honours degree programmes in social work should be designed to help students learn to become accountable, reflective, critical and evaluative. This involves learning to:

- think critically about the complex social, legal, economic, political and cultural contexts in which social work practice is located;

- work in a transparent and responsible way, balancing autonomy with complex, multiple and sometimes contradictory accountabilities (for example, to different service users, employing agencies, professional bodies and the wider society);

- exercise authority within complex frameworks of accountability and ethical and legal boundaries;

- acquire and apply the habits of critical reflection, self-evaluation and consultation, and make appropriate use of research in decision-making about practice and in the evaluation of outcomes.

5 Subject knowledge, understanding and skills

Subject knowledge and understanding

5.1 During their degree studies in social work, honours graduates should acquire, critically evaluate, apply and integrate knowledge and understanding in the following five core areas of study.

5.1.1 **Social work services, service users and carers**, which include:

- the social processes (associated with, for example, poverty, migration, unemployment, poor health, disablement, lack of education and other sources of disadvantage) that lead to marginalisation, isolation and exclusion, and their impact on the demand for social work services;

- explanations of the links between definitional processes contributing to social differences (for example, social class, gender, ethnic differences, age, sexuality and religious belief) to the problems of inequality and differential need faced by service users;

- the nature of social work services in a diverse society (with particular reference to concepts such as prejudice, interpersonal, institutional and structural discrimination, empowerment and anti-discriminatory practices);

- the nature and validity of different definitions of, and explanations for, the characteristics and circumstances of service users and the services required by them, drawing on knowledge from research, practice experience, and from service users and carers;

- the focus on outcomes, such as promoting the wellbeing of young people and their families, and promoting dignity, choice and independence for adults receiving services;

- the relationship between agency policies, legal requirements and professional boundaries in shaping the nature of services provided in interdisciplinary contexts and the issues associated with working across professional boundaries and within different disciplinary groups.

5.1.2 **The service delivery context**, which includes:

- the location of contemporary social work within historical, comparative and global perspectives, including European and international contexts;

- the changing demography and cultures of communities in which social workers will be practising;

- the complex relationships between public, social and political philosophies, policies and priorities and the organisation and practice of social work, including the contested nature of these;

- the issues and trends in modern public and social policy and their relationship to contemporary practice and service delivery in social work;

- the significance of legislative and legal frameworks and service delivery standards (including the nature of legal authority, the application of legislation in practice, statutory accountability and tensions between statute, policy and practice);

- the current range and appropriateness of statutory, voluntary and private agencies providing community-based, day-care, residential and other services and the organisational systems inherent within these;

- the significance of interrelationships with other related services, including housing, health, income maintenance and criminal justice (where not an integral social service);

- the contribution of different approaches to management, leadership and quality in public and independent human services;

- the development of personalised services, individual budgets and direct payments;

- the implications of modern information and communications technology (ICT) for both the provision and receipt of services.

5.1.3 **Values and ethics**, which include:

- the nature, historical evolution and application of social work values;

- the moral concepts of rights, responsibility, freedom, authority and power inherent in the practice of social workers as moral and statutory agents;

- the complex relationships between justice, care and control in social welfare and the practical and ethical implications of these, including roles as statutory agents and in upholding the law in respect of discrimination;

- aspects of philosophical ethics relevant to the understanding and resolution of value dilemmas and conflicts in both interpersonal and professional contexts;

- the conceptual links between codes defining ethical practice, the regulation of professional conduct and the management of potential conflicts generated by the codes held by different professional groups.

5.1.4 **Social work theory**, which includes:

- research-based concepts and critical explanations from social work theory and other disciplines that contribute to the knowledge base of social work, including their distinctive epistemological status and application to practice;

- the relevance of sociological perspectives to understanding societal and structural influences on human behaviour at individual, group and community levels;

- the relevance of psychological, physical and physiological perspectives to understanding personal and social development and functioning;

- social science theories explaining group and organisational behaviour, adaptation and change;

- models and methods of assessment, including factors underpinning the selection and testing of relevant information, the nature of professional judgement and the processes of risk assessment and decision-making;

- approaches and methods of intervention in a range of settings, including factors guiding the choice and evaluation of these;

- user-led perspectives;

- knowledge and critical appraisal of relevant social research and evaluation methodologies, and the evidence base for social work.

5.1.5 **The nature of social work practice**, which includes:

- the characteristics of practice in a range of community-based and organisational settings within statutory, voluntary and private sectors, and the factors influencing changes and developments in practice within these contexts;

- the nature and characteristics of skills associated with effective practice, both direct and indirect, with a range of service-users and in a variety of settings;

- the processes that facilitate and support service user choice and independence;

- the factors and processes that facilitate effective interdisciplinary, interprofessional and interagency collaboration and partnership;

- the place of theoretical perspectives and evidence from international research in assessment and decision-making processes in social work practice;

- the integration of theoretical perspectives and evidence from international research into the design and implementation of effective social work intervention, with a wide range of service users, carers and others;

- the processes of reflection and evaluation, including familiarity with the range of approaches for evaluating service and welfare outcomes, and their significance for the development of practice and the practitioner.

Problem-solving skills

5.5 These are sub-divided into four areas.

5.5.1 **Managing problem-solving activities:** honours graduates in social work should be able to plan problem-solving activities, i.e. to:

- think logically, systematically, critically and reflectively;

- apply ethical principles and practices critically in planning problem-solving activities;

- plan a sequence of actions to achieve specified objectives, making use of research, theory and other forms of evidence;

- manage processes of change, drawing on research, theory and other forms of evidence.

5.5.2 **Gathering information:** honours graduates in social work should be able to:

- gather information from a wide range of sources and by a variety of methods, for a range of purposes. These methods should include electronic searches, reviews of relevant literature, policy and procedures, face-to-face interviews, written and telephone contact with individuals and groups;

- take into account differences of viewpoint in gathering information and critically assess the reliability and relevance of the information gathered;

- assimilate and disseminate relevant information in reports and case records.

5.5.3 **Analysis and synthesis:** honours graduates in social work should be able to analyse and synthesise knowledge gathered for problem-solving purposes, i.e. to:

- assess human situations, taking into account a variety of factors (including the views of participants, theoretical concepts, research evidence, legislation and organisational policies and procedures);

- analyse information gathered, weighing competing evidence and modifying their viewpoint in light of new information, then relate this information to a particular task, situation or problem;

- consider specific factors relevant to social work practice (such as risk, rights, cultural differences and linguistic sensitivities, responsibilities to protect vulnerable individuals and legal obligations);

- assess the merits of contrasting theories, explanations, research, policies and procedures;

- synthesise knowledge and sustain reasoned argument;

- employ a critical understanding of human agency at the macro (societal), mezzo (organisational and community) and micro (inter and intrapersonal) levels;

- critically analyse and take account of the impact of inequality and discrimination in work with people in particular contexts and problem situations.

5.5.4 **Intervention and evaluation:** honours graduates in social work should be able to use their knowledge of a range of interventions and evaluation processes selectively to:

- build and sustain purposeful relationships with people and organisations in community-based, and interprofessional contexts;

- make decisions, set goals and construct specific plans to achieve these, taking into account relevant factors including ethical guidelines;

- negotiate goals and plans with others, analysing and addressing in a creative manner human, organisational and structural impediments to change;

- implement plans through a variety of systematic processes that include working in partnership;

- undertake practice in a manner that promotes the well-being and protects the safety of all parties;

- engage effectively in conflict resolution;

- support service users to take decisions and access services, with the social worker as navigator, advocate and supporter;

- manage the complex dynamics of dependency and, in some settings, provide direct care and personal support in everyday living situations;

- meet deadlines and comply with external definitions of a task;

- plan, implement and critically review processes and outcomes;

- bring work to an effective conclusion, taking into account the implications for all involved;

- monitor situations, review processes and evaluate outcomes;

- use and evaluate methods of intervention critically and reflectively.

Communication skills

5.6 Honours graduates in social work should be able to communicate clearly, accurately and precisely (in an appropriate medium) with individuals and groups in a range of formal and informal situations, i.e. to:

- make effective contact with individuals and organisations for a range of objectives, by verbal, paper-based and electronic means;

- clarify and negotiate the purpose of such contacts and the boundaries of their involvement;

- listen actively to others, engage appropriately with the life experiences of service users, understand accurately their viewpoint and overcome personal prejudices to respond appropriately to a range of complex personal and interpersonal situations;

- use both verbal and non-verbal cues to guide interpretation;

- identify and use opportunities for purposeful and supportive communication with service users within their everyday living situations;

- follow and develop an argument and evaluate the viewpoints of, and evidence presented by, others;

- write accurately and clearly in styles adapted to the audience, purpose and context of the communication;

- use advocacy skills to promote others' rights, interests and needs;

- present conclusions verbally and on paper, in a structured form, appropriate to the audience for which these have been prepared;

- make effective preparation for, and lead meetings in a productive way;

- communicate effectively across potential barriers resulting from differences (for example, in culture, language and age).

Skills in working with others

5.7 Honours graduates in social work should be able to work effectively with others, i.e. to:

- involve users of social work services in ways that increase their resources, capacity and power to influence factors affecting their lives;

- consult actively with others, including service users and carers, who hold relevant information or expertise;

- act co-operatively with others, liaising and negotiating across differences such as organisational and professional boundaries and differences of identity or language;

- develop effective helping relationships and partnerships with other individuals, groups and organisations that facilitate change;

- act with others to increase social justice by identifying and responding to prejudice, institutional discrimination and structural inequality;

- act within a framework of multiple accountability (for example, to agencies, the public, service users, carers and others);

- challenge others when necessary, in ways that are most likely to produce positive outcomes.

Skills in personal and professional development

5.8 Honours graduates in social work should be able to:

- advance their own learning and understanding with a degree of independence;

- reflect on and modify their behaviour in the light of experience;

- identify and keep under review their own personal and professional boundaries;

- manage uncertainty, change and stress in work situations;

- handle inter and intrapersonal conflict constructively;

- understand and manage changing situations and respond in a flexible manner;

- challenge unacceptable practices in a responsible manner;

- take responsibility for their own further and continuing acquisition and use of knowledge and skills;

- use research critically and effectively to sustain and develop their practice.

6 Teaching, learning and assessment

6.2 The learning processes in social work at honours degree level can be expressed in terms of four interrelated themes.

- **Awareness raising, skills and knowledge acquisition** – a process in which the student becomes more aware of aspects of knowledge and expertise, learns how to systematically engage with and acquire new areas of knowledge, recognises their potential and becomes motivated to engage in new ways of thinking and acting.

- **Conceptual understanding** – a process in which a student acquires, examines critically and deepens understanding (measured and tested against existing knowledge and adjustments made in attitudes and goals).

- **Practice skills and experience** – processes in which a student learns practice skills in the contexts identified in paragraph 4.4 and applies theoretical models and research evidence together with new understanding to relevant activities, and receives feedback from various sources on performance, enhancing openness to critical self-evaluation.

- **Reflection on performance** – a process in which a student reflects critically and evaluatively on past experience, recent performance, and feedback, and applies this information to the process of integrating awareness (including awareness of the impact of self on others) and new understanding, leading to improved performance.

Index